BETWEEN THE TRACKS

Walks Around Sheffield's Super Tram Network

BETWEEN THE TRACKS

Walks in the spaces around Sheffield's Super Tram Network

Colin Richards

Banister Publications Ltd
118 Saltergate
Chesterfield
Derbyshire S40 1NG

First published in Great Britain in 2012 by

Bannister Publications Ltd
118 Saltergate
Chesterfield
Derbyshire S40 1NG

ISBN 978-0-9572074-0-0

A catalogue record for this book is available from the British Library

Typeset and cover designed by Escritor Design
Chesterfield, Derbyshire

Printed and bound in the UK by the MPG Books Group,
Bodmin and King's Lynn

1 Halfway to Birley Lane

2 Meadowhall to Wincobank Hill Round Walk

3 Middlewood to Halfway

4 Herding/Leighton to White Lane

5 Halfway to Meadowhall

6 Halfway to Waterthorpe

7 Meadowhall to Middlewood

8 Cathedral to University

9 Shalesmoor to Hillsborough Park

10 Woodbourn Rd to Carbrook

11 Malin Bridge Round Walk

12 Herdings to Granville Rd

CONTENTS

Page	Walk	Route	Miles	Km	Hours
1	Walk 1	Halfway to Birley Lane	5	8	2½
7	Walk 2	Meadowhall Interchange via Wincobank Hill Fort	2½	4	1½
13	Walk 3	Middlewood to Halfway	22	35	10
41	Walk 4	Herdings/Leighton Rd to White Lane	3	5	1½
45	Walk 5	Halfway to Meadowhall	12	19	4½
53	Walk 6	Halfway to Waterthorpe via Rother Valley Park	4	6	1½
57	Walk 7	Meadowhall to Middlewood	7	11	3
65	Walk 8	Cathedral to University	1½	2½	1
75	Walk 9	Shalesmoor to Hillsborough Park	4	6½	2½
83	Walk 10	Woodbourn Rd to Carbrook	3½	5½	2
89	Walk 11	Malin Bridge/Rivelin/Loxley Round Walk	4	6½	2
95	Walk 12	Herdings Park to Granville Road	5	8	2½
101	Walk 13	Meadowhall to Meadowhall Challenge	41	65	18

INTRODUCTION

Sheffield had an extensive network of first-generation trams in the 19th Century. The first tram ran in 1873, and electric trams began operation in 1899. At its greatest extent, 100 miles of tram routes were operated by Sheffield Corporation.

They were a popular way of getting about in a city known as the 'City of Seven Hills'. The city centre lies in a valley, which was also home to the steel mills and other heavy industry with its need for water. Many of the suburbs and surrounding districts are on the hills overlooking the city. Early motor buses struggled with the gradients, and the railways were only able to serve the valley meaning that no proper local railway network developed as in other major cities. Tramways were the ideal way to overcome the steep gradients and provide a local transport service.

As with all British cities, trams fell out of favour in the 1950s and 60s. Sheffield's last tram ran in 1960, at which time the system was one of only a handful left in the UK.

A replacement, modern light rail system was proposed in the early 1970s and eventually authorised by a Parliamentary Bill in 1985. Subsequent alterations and associated public consultation exercises delayed the start of the project, but in 1991 construction on the Sheffield Supertram finally started.

The first line to be built was Line Two to Meadowhall, which, after leaving the city centre, is entirely off-street. It opened for passengers on 23 March 1994 and the final section, Shalesmoor–Middlewood and Malin Bridge, opened on 23 October 1995. There are 18 miles of track, 48 stations and the network cost around £240 million to build.

I've been travelling on the network since its early days and still enjoy the experience and the opportunity to see much of Sheffield from unfamiliar angles. Views and scenes taken for granted for years take on a new lease of life. Another aspect is that the route of the tram network passes through a whole range of social, geographic and economic areas, with the tram stops offering a chance to pause and enjoy many of the different elements which make up our fair city.

For me and, I believe, for most folk, the tram system is fun to use. I've tried to reflect this in the walks in this book. There are thirteen, all deliberately light hearted, except perhaps Walk No. 13, which is set as a challenge for the strongest walkers out there.

I've included snippets of information about many of the fascinating things you see along the way, as a prompt for those who may be interested in learning more, but for consistency of approach, none of them go into too much detail. An easy way to delve into the facts, figures and the history of these places is through the Internet. I've included references in each walk and have included 'Quick Response Codes' (QR Codes) so that those with smart phones can easily access some websites of interest whilst walking. We live in a world of miracles!

The maps are just to give a flavour for each walk. All the detailed directions are in the text. You may also find Ordnance Survey Pathfinder Maps 726, 743 and 744 and/or a street map of Sheffield a useful addition. If you're not somewhere on one of these, you're badly off course!

I would like to thank Warren Hayes, who kindly tested all the walks to ensure that the directions given in the book correspond to the paths, marks and features on the ground. Transforming notes, photographs and maps into a book is more complex than I imagined and I should also like to thank my publisher, Tom Blyth, for his help and advice in producing this book.

The maps I have used are reproduced and adapted by kind permission of www.openstreetmap.org and www.creativecommons.org.

I hope you enjoy the walks as much as I have.

Colin Richards

WALK ONE
HALFWAY TO BIRLEY LANE

Description

A varied walk, initially through pleasant suburbia then farm and woodland and back via the golf course. Mostly gentle walking with occasional longer climbs.

Start: Halfway Tram Terminus

Finish: Birley Lane Tram Stop

Distance:
5 miles/8 km

Time:
Allow 2½ hrs

I

Directions

Walk away from the tram towards the roundabout. Carry straight across and up the road towards Eckington. On the brow of the hill, just before the next roundabout, turn right into School Avenue.

In 50 metres keep straight on the path between the hedges. Carry on up with, at first the new estate and then, the school field on the left with houses on right. The path eventually meets Halfway Drive just before the Double Top pub.

Turn left onto Halfway Drive, left into Malham Grove and then right into Malham Gardens. Take the path on the left up into the top corner of the estate. The path then leads between the houses into a field. Keeping to the path, sweep left, then down, to a road 50 metres below the George and Dragon pub.

Mosborough Methodist Church

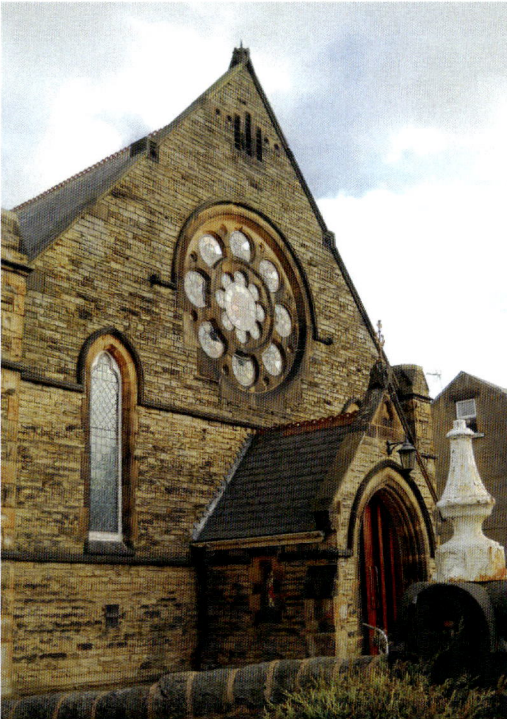

At the road, turn right, then left, up Duke Street. As the road splits at the white railings, take the right option down to a T-junction. Turn right down Chapel Street passing the Mosborough Methodist Church on your right. Turn left at the end into Plumbley Hall road. Veer left just before the Wheel pub and then left again into Marsh Close. Head for the path to open fields between the houses in the far right corner. We are now in open country.

Cross the field then left down the edge of the next field, turning right along the bottom (don't go over the stile). Carry along the bottom of this field, and drop down the steps into a sunken track. Turn left down to the wood for 100 metres to a crossroads. Ahead you see the welcome "Keep Out, No Road" painted in white on the trees in front. Heeding this friendly advice, turn right, then immediately left, over a stile into a field. Follow the path along the edge of the field, skirting the wood on your left.

The path eventually starts to climb. After about another 100 metres, turn left over the stile in the fence into the woods, down the path to the Moss stream at the bottom. Turn right over a cast iron stile, ignoring the white footbridge on the left. Carry straight on for only 20 metres, then take the stile and track which leads diagonally up the right hand side of the fishing pond towards Bushes Wood and the lane.

At the lane, turn left along it. After a short way it climbs up, then down into a dip in the trees. In this dip, turn right over a stile at the side of a gate and start up the hill (it's quite a long climb). Head for the top right hand corner of the field to the stile. Over the stile turn left then stop. Pause to get

...over a stile and into the field

Intriguing inscription on this spring head

your breath and enjoy the view over Moss Valley. Remember, you've caught the tram to here.

After your rest, go left down the hill, right over the stile down to a metal footbridge, last concreted in 1945 (if you can find the "inscription"underfoot).

Turn right up the hill. In 30 metres take the lower, right hand stile into the field. Keep on the right edge of the field and carry on through 3 more, much smaller fields and over a stile. Here you have a choice. If you like a challenge, carry on up in the same direction (but first have a quick look at the intriguing spring just down to the right which has been suitably commemorated by the local Ridgeway village folk). This usually requires battling through the currently, extremely overgrown area, over the next stile in the far corner and then sharp left up the path between the gardens to the road. If it looks impenetrable, turn left up the side of the fence to the road and turn right. In either case you'll soon see the primary school on the right, with the Queens Head over the road. Turn right up the hill to the T- junction.

Turn right for 50 metres. You'll see High Lane farm house down to your right. Immediately opposite on other side of the road is the path we're looking for. Take this path, first up (admiring the sudden views again) and then down to towards the wood. Turn diagonally left up through the wood. The track comes out just past the electricity pylon. Keeping an eye out for golf balls, cross the course under the power lines. As the track turns up to the clubhouse, go

Further Information on this Walk

Mosborough Community:

http://www.abdecor.co.uk/mosborough/

The Ridgeway Village

http://www.ridgewayvillage.org.uk

straight on the short distance up to Birley Lane. Turn left up to the tram stop, which ends this walk.

Meadowhall, spread out in all its splendour

onto a narrow track behind the houses. The Meadowhall Shopping Centre (opened in 1990 on the site of one of Sheffield's largest steelworks) is spread out in all its splendour directly below.

Turn left and along here is probably the best view in Sheffield of the complete Tinsley viaduct from end to end. An excellent piece of civil engineering built in the mid-1960s but requiring frequent upgrading over the years. Nevertheless, it's worth a minute's study.

Carry on straight down, with the houses on the left, factory units on the right, ignoring all the turn offs along the way, until eventually the track meets the road. Turn right and right again into Evesham Close. Walk down to the bottom taking the path between houses Nos. 22 & 24. Cross the road and turn right for 100 metres to the footpath on the left, leading back to Meadowhall Interchange and the tram stop.

Further Information on this Walk

The Wentworth Follies:

http://www.inkamera.ukgo.com/wfolly/index.htm

Wincobank Hill:

https://www.sheffield.gov.uk/out--about/parks-woodlands--countryside/trees--woodlands/woodland-sites-and-projects/wincobank-hill.html

WALK THREE
MIDDLEWOOD TO HALFWAY

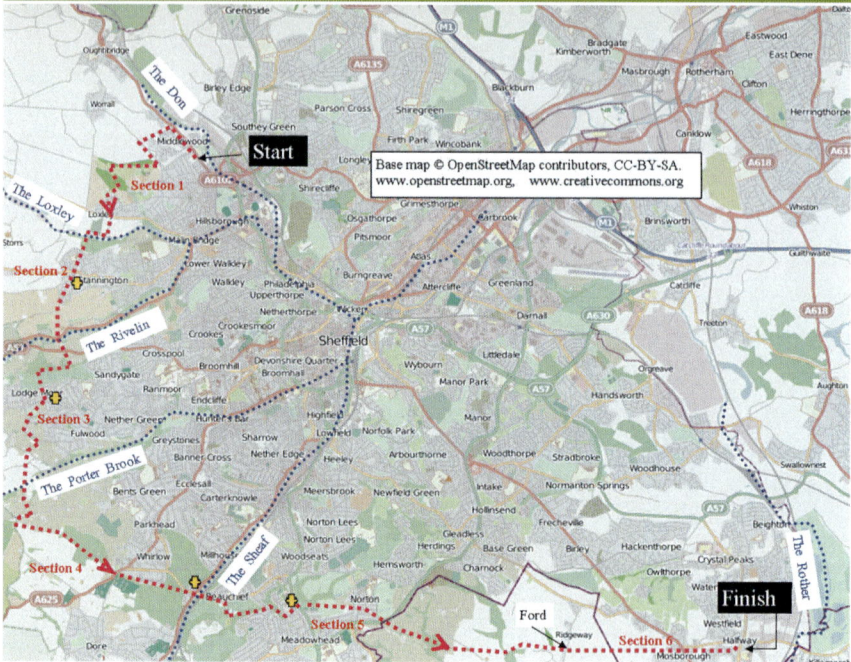

Base map © OpenStreetMap contributors, CC-BY-SA.
www.openstreetmap.org,   www.creativecommons.org

Description

Without doubt, this is the 'Big One'. Not for the faint hearted, it traverses six river valleys as it skirts around the west and south of Sheffield. It covers a whole range of walking experience from suburbia, through farmland, woodland and across ancient commons.

It runs through river valleys, up gruelling climbs, along spectacular edges and relaxing long gentle descents. It goes through parks, golf courses and secluded backwaters. It's truly a gem but be warned: it's not for the beginner or the less active.

Distance:
22 miles/35 km

Time:
Allow 10 hrs

13

So that the directions don't get too tedious, the walk is divided into six sections based on the rivers you will encounter. There are, however, many well-served public transport routes along the way for those who might wish to do the walk in sections. These are marked in the text with this symbol:

and on the maps with this symbol:

Start: Middlewood Tram Terminus

Finish: Halfway Tram Terminus

The Sections:

Section 1: River Don to River Loxley

Section 2: River Loxley to River Rivelin

Section 3: River Rivelin to Porter Brook

Section 4: Porter Brook to River Sheaf

Section 5: River Sheaf to Ford

Section 6: Ford to Halfway

SECTION 1: RIVER DON TO RIVER LOXLEY

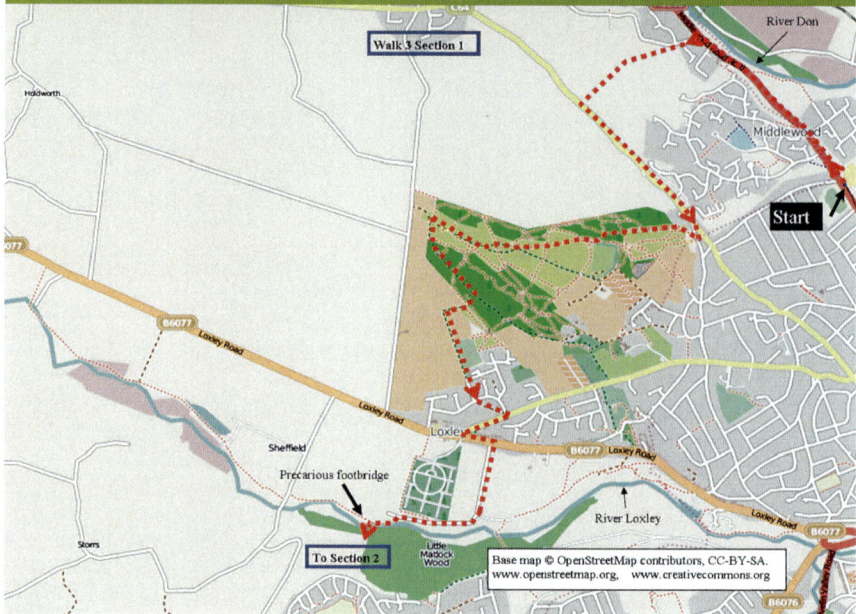

Directions

After getting off the tram, walk away from the city towards Oughtibridge with the River Don out of sight down on the right and past the new housing estate on the site of Middlewood Hospital on your left. Carry on past the new Health Centre on the left and after passing some more new housing on the left, eventually turn left up Stockarth Lane. In 50 metres, opposite Rowburn Drive, take the footpath on the left, signposted 'To Worrall'. The path gradually climbs along the edge of the field up to Worrall Road. At the road turn left and walk on, enjoying the views while you get your breath back: there's plenty more of this to come.

The Section

Distance:
4 miles/
6.5 km

Time:
Allow 1½hrs

15

Entrance to the Old Middlewood Hospital

Carry on down for about 1km, passing Queenswood Road and Dykewood Drive on the left. Just further on at the end of the cottages on the right, turn right up Rural Lane and then immediately right again at the footpath sign about 20 metres further on. Take the right hand path along the back of the cottages.

Keeping to the right hand path, follow the signs. After 50 metres, at the end of the gardens, the sign points diagonally away from cottages up through an area of young trees with the remains of a wall on your left, beyond which are heather, gorse and bilberry bushes.

Continue up until the path crosses this derelict wall and then, further on, meets another path coming up from the left with the remains of another wall slightly to the left. Cross the broken wall again and turn right. This uneven, rocky path eventually reaches the crest.

Turn right again up the crest, as views from the left now start to emerge as you travel along Loxley Common,- arguably an old stomping ground of a certain Robin Hood. Head up the hill and as you reach the brow, you'll see a gate and a small parking area. Continue ahead and in 50 metres, just before the stone gate posts, turn left down the bridleway heading down into Loxley valley.

The path leads straight ahead and down through the trees for 200 metres. As it splits, take the signposted right hand fork out into farmland over a stile. Go straight on, with the wall on the right, to another stile and gate. Turn immediately left down to the houses along a lovely grass track with views to the right to Loxley and towards Bradfield.

The path leads out into France Road. Carry on down across the road into the old and curious Occupation Lane, which leads between the backs of the houses to Chase Road. Turn right and immediately right again down Rodney Hill.

Just before the junction, turn left across the grass onto Loxley Road and then, after 50 metres, turn right down Black Lane, passing a sports field on your left (where, incidentally, I spent many years pretending to be a goalkeeper).

At the bottom, turn right past a row of cottages on your left and the cemetery on your right, heading towards Olive Mill. Just before the buildings in front of Olive House, turn left as signposted through the yard and round the back to the dam with the picturesque Olive House now on the far side.

Halfway along the dam, turn left over the River Loxley across a somewhat precarious footbridge. Just pausing for a while and taking in the peace and quiet of the area, it's difficult to imagine that death and destruction on a huge scale swept past this spot in 1864.

... a somewhat precarious footbridge on the Sheffield flood route

That was when Dale Dyke dam further up the valley burst, sending a tidal wave of water rolling down all the way to the centre of town, drowning well over 250 poor souls on the way. It left a trail of destruction, devastating everything in its path. At this spot the wall of water would have been well over 20 feet high. Anyway enough of this misery, let's get on to the next challenge.

Further Information on this Walk

Robin Hood of Loxley:

http://www.robinhoodloxley.net/mycustompage0037.htm

Loxley, South Yorkshire:

http://en.wikipedia.org/wiki/Loxley,_South_Yorkshire

The Sheffield Floods:

https://www.sheffield.gov.uk/libraries/archives-and-local-studies/publications/sheffield-flood.html

SECTION 2: RIVER LOXLEY TO RIVER RIVELIN

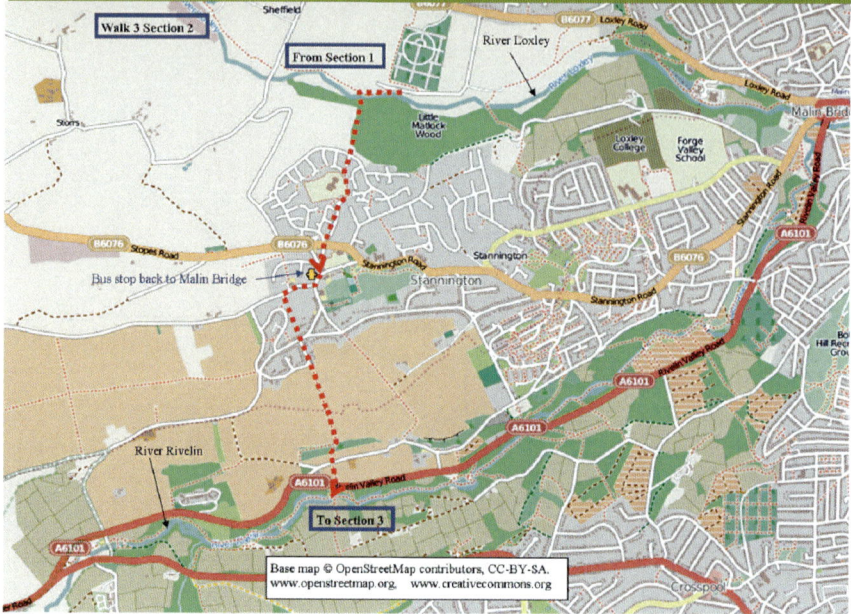

Base map © OpenStreetMap contributors, CC-BY-SA.
www.openstreetmap.org, www.creativecommons.org

Directions

Having crossed the River Loxley, the path turns to the left up a few steps. At the top of the steps, turn immediately right. The plan is to go straight up from here, ignoring any temptation to take easier detours. This is a little gruelling but well worth it at the top.

Climb the hill, keeping the fence close on your right. It is a less well defined and steeper path than some others but don't weaken. Carry on up. Just before the top, have another breather and a look back.

When recovered, climb up to the road, turn left and then immediately right up Oak Apple Walk through the new estate

The Section

Distance:
2 miles/
2.5 km

Time:
Allow 1½ hrs

19

of houses up past Nook Lane School on your right. Carry on up Nook Lane, left onto Acorn Drive and then across the next road up past the bollards to Sheldon Lane with the Rose and Crown on your right. Go up Bankfield Lane turning right and then right again up on to Uppergate Road.

There is a bus stop here for the frequent SL2 back down to Malin Bridge tram stop, if the climb has been a bit too exhausting and the prospect of two more substantial hills to climb is a little daunting.

Just past the Crown and Glove take the path on the left down the back of the houses to the junction. Take Nethergate opposite. As it bends to the right past the Old School house, take the path directly in front down towards Rivelin Valley. Opposite, you are looking at the next challenge. Carry on down through open fields, then a short steep hill down to an iron post. Go down this somewhat overgrown section across a lane and down another

...have another breather and a look back

overgrown section to the main road. Go straight across and down a cobbled path to the River Rivelin over the footbridge.

Opposite, you're looking at the next challenge

Further Information on this Walk

Stannington Village:
http://en.wikipedia.org/wiki/Stannington

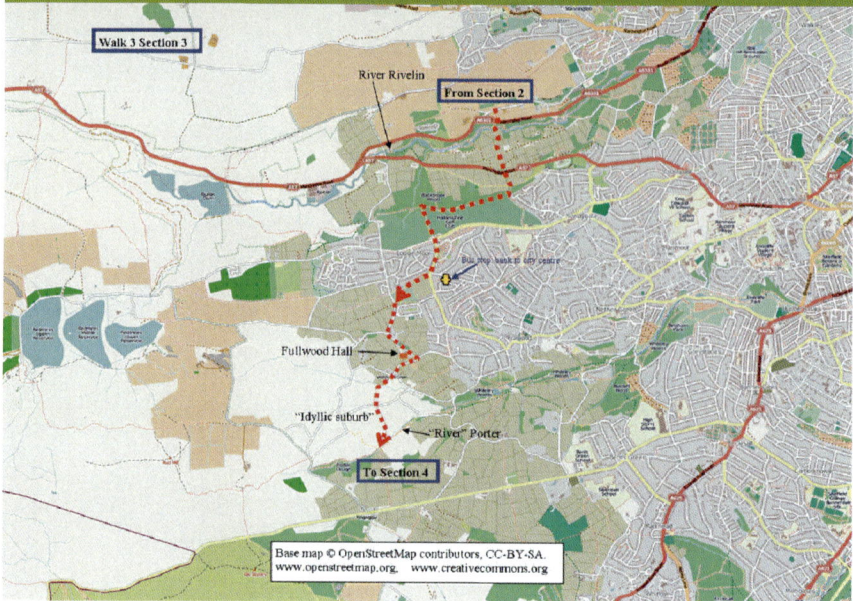

SECTION 3: RIVER RIVELIN TO PORTER BROOK

Directions

From the footbridge over the River Rivelin carry on up the hill, keeping the ruined wall immediately on your right.

Go through several fields, across Manchester Road and up the next 2 fields directly opposite. You now reach an old track known as Coppice Road. Turn left and then immediately right up into the wood.

Climb this steep, rock strewn path, keeping the small brook on your right,to the top turning right along the edge with the boundary wall of Hallamshire Golf Club on your left and absolutely stunning views out to the right. Well worth the climb. Walk along the ridge for about half a kilometre, enjoying

Distance:
3 miles/
5 km

Time:
Allow 1½ hrs

23

the views (and the novelty of a relatively horizontal path with only a few short steep gullies to negotiate). Eventually you reach a legitimate break in the wall (please ignore the illegal one just before) with stone steps leading up to a path across the golf course. You'll see the official warning sign as you enter. Take this path (keeping an eye out for golf balls and golfers) up and over the course keeping between the blue marker sticks. It comes out opposite the Shiny Sheff pub.

Cross the road and go up Crimicar Lane, passing the gates to the old Crimicar Hospital on your left. Just over the brow, (120 bus stop just along Barncliffe Road to the left) take the path to the right around the edge of the sports ground past a playground to Blackbrook road. Turn left up this road and then left down Harrison Lane, with great views over Mayfield valley.

Keeping to the raised path on the left gives you an opportunity to admire the stone roof tiles and mullion windows of the lovely Fullwood Hall as you pass. As you

...absolutely stunning views

24

The idyllic suburb of the Mayfield Valley

reach David Lane, just round the bend, turn right down the hill past the old school house to the T-junction at the bottom.

Take Green Lane opposite, past some lovely little cottages and over a stream, up some steps and through a wooden gate into a field. At the far end turn left along the road then immediately right up onto a stile and along the grassy path to the right of Old May House.

Looking to the left towards the city centre in the distance you can only agree that this must surely be one of Sheffield's most idyllic suburbs. Climb the next wooden stile, go straight across a field and the path now descends to meet the Sheffield Round Walk. Climb over the stile and, immediately ahead, go through the wall gap and turn left along the track over the (River) Porter Brook.

Further Information on this Walk

The National Archives, Crimicar Hospital:
http://www.nationalarchives.gov.uk/A2A/records.aspx?cat=199-nhs14&cid=0#0

SECTION 4: PORTER BROOK TO RIVER SHEAF

Base map © OpenStreetMap contributors, CC-BY-SA.
www.openstreetmap.org,   www.creativecommons.org

Directions

Just round the corner from the track over the Porter Brook, take the sign-posted path on the right over the stile and straight up the middle of the field. Although this is steep, I can promise you that it's the last challenge for some time and that the next few kilometres will be extremely relaxing.

At the top, carry on through a couple of fields to the road on the horizon. Turn right at the road up past the Norfolk Arms and then left along Sheephill Lane in front of the Round House (shaped such that the toll keeper could keep an eye on the several roads meeting here).

The Section

Distance:
3.5 miles/ 5.5 km

Time:
Allow 1½ hrs

27

At the dip in the road turn left over the stile into the field towards the Limb valley. Go down the field, across the relatively new section through the boggy surroundings.

Ignore the sign to the right and go past the derelict Copperas house on your right. 'Copperas' (ferrous sulphate) was manufactured here from the pyritic Ringinglow Coal seam, mined nearby. The copperas solution was used in the leather tanning industry.

Also ignore the next sign to the right, and take the path just a little further on and then turn right, through the small gate, down the steps into the wooded Limb Valley.

The path meanders with twists and turns and ups and downs for about 1.5km until you reach a junction where a stone bridge gives you an option to take a path to the right into Whirlow Brook Park. Ignore this option and carry on straight ahead, first up and then down, past the pond and to the road.

Turn right past the entrance to Whirlow Park and out to the main road. Go straight across and drop down the little steep slope out to the left hand side of the playing fields opposite.

The Round House

28

Derelict Copperas House

Keeping to the left edge of the field (or slightly further along, take the second small track left into the trees if you like a bit of shade).

Carry on down to the bottom and through the narrow gap in the wall. Walk down into the woods with the stream on the left. After about 25 metres, take the left fork keeping the stream on your left. Trip over the tree roots and stumble down to, and over a wooden bridge.

Turn left up the cobbles and steps. At the top, with a five bar gate on your left, turn right and then left carrying on down the main path, keeping just inside the edge of the wood. On the right you can just see the boundary fence of the bird sanctuary, and on the left you pass the backs of some gardens. At the end of the gardens, carry on straight down. After about another 30 metres at the next fork, ignore the sign, and take the right fork.

The track curves right and left all the way down until eventually you'll see the gate ahead out into Abbey Lane. Turn right down to the lights (buses back to the city centre), then straight up opposite, over the River Sheaf.

Further Information on this Walk

Ringinglow Round House:

http://www.bbc.co.uk/southyorkshire/content/articles/2008/08/01/round_house_ringinglow_road_feature.shtml

The Friends of Porter Valley:

http://www.sheffieldportervalley.org.uk/index.html

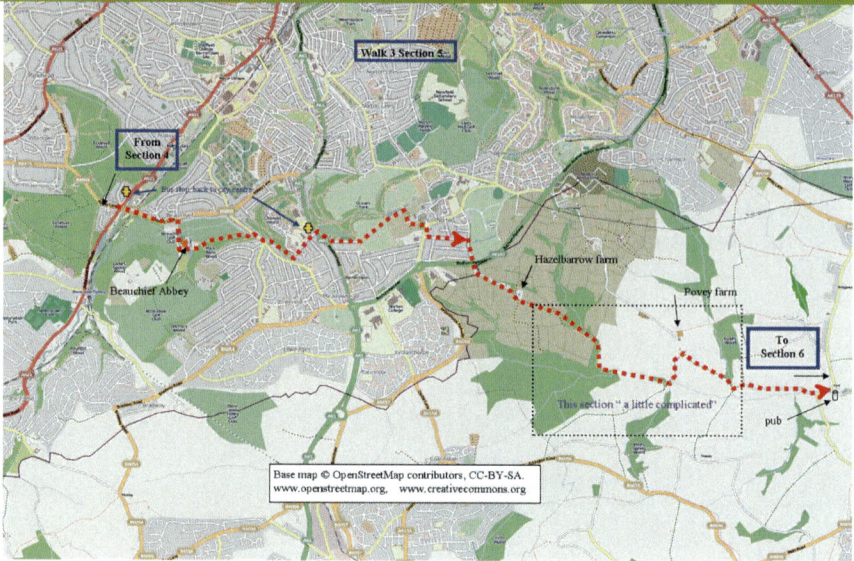

SECTION 5: RIVER SHEAF TO FORD

Directions

The Section

Continue away from the River Sheaf, over the railway, past the entrance to Beauchief Golf Course and up for about 400 metres to Beauchief Abbey Lane. As you walk up this stretch, note the parallel service road in front of the houses opposite. That is part of the original tram track route from the distant past. Turn right along Beauchief Abbey Lane with the golf course on your left, up past the cottages and the historic Beauchief Abbey itself (founded in 1183 and still going strong today). This setting is probably the most photographed, sketched and painted scene in the whole of Sheffield.

Just past the Abbey turn left as you re-join a section of the Round Walk to Parkbank Wood.

**Distance:
6 miles/
10.5 km**

**Time:
Allow 2½
hrs**

Beauchief Abbey, a popular photo choice

Carry on up past the ponds into the wood all the way straight up with the tenth fairway immediately on your left. The path leads gently up towards the houses in the distance and then veers upwards, right behind them to a sharp left hand turn that takes you down between the houses, to Bocking Lane.

Cross the busy road, turn right and walk for 100 metres, then go left opposite the junction down into Chancet Wood, between the houses. At the bottom of the path, cross the stream and take the right hand fork up the slope and further up another, unmarked, right hand fork to emerge on Chancet Wood Drive.

Turn left here and then go straight up the hill past the school and the bollards at the top, heading towards the trees of Graves Park directly in front.

Cross the busy Chesterfield Road (last chance for a frequent bus service back to the city centre) and go into the park. Turn right up the path with the mini golf pitch and putt on your left. Follow the path up past the bowling greens and tennis courts to the car

parking area at the top gates. Here, the route staggers slightly right and then left.

...through the avenue of trees to the old boating pond

Take the left fork ahead, up through the avenue of commemorative trees to the old boating pond. Carry on the path with the pond on your left to the far end. At the end of the first pond turn right up the path away from the ponds, with the metal railing on your left, towards the rare breeds enclosures.

Just over the brow of the hill turn left past the old Norton Hall (the seat of the estate of which Graves park was but a part) out towards Norton Lane and the Chantry obelisk (erected in homage to Sir Francis Chantry a famous Georgian sculptor, buried here in what was then a Derbyshire, village). You should just catch glimpses of the lovely Norton Church through the trees as you leave the park.

At the road, turn right down Norton lane, then left into Henley Avenue. You should spot the many excellent art deco houses along the way. At the end, turn right down School Lane past Brocklehurst Avenue to the bend. At the bend take the bridle path directly in front and cross the dual carriageway (beware of the fast moving traffic).

...down past the farm yard

Go down the track opposite heading towards Hazelbarrow Farm, passing some old kennels on your left.

At Hazelbarrow farm, take the right hand track down past the farm yard and cottage. Go through the left hand gate, straight ahead and straight on, out into the field, keeping to the right hand edge all the way down. Go through or over the next gate and down through the field to the edge of the trees.

This next section gets a little complicated. Carry on along the track along the bottom of the field and, just after entering the trees, take the track off to the left into Newfield Spring Wood, as signposted. You should be walking with a gully on your left and a field away up to the right. The path eventually breaks back out to the edge of the field.

Carry on, and as the path drops down into the corner, turn left over the footbridge. Go up the slope for no more than 5 metres and then take the right fork up the path along the edge of a fenced field for about 50 metres until you see two stone gate posts on the right. Turn right through these into the wood and carry on. You should now see a field on the left and a gully on the right.

The path now descends to join another. Turn left at this junction down towards the stream. Cross the stream as best you can and carry on up the other side through the wood. It's usually a little churned up round here.

Go up through the pine trees, keeping left along the edge of the next field and, after about 30 metres, turn left again at the corner into the trees. You quickly emerge along the edge of another field. Go through the next gap into yet another field and down to, and over, a footbridge on the left over a stream. Just to check you're still on the right path, at this point you should be about to pass underneath some electricity cables.

Carry on with the stream on your right over the next footbridge and then right through the wood to meet Owler Carr Lane (merely a track). Turn left down to the ford and either carry straight across and up the other side or, if you prefer dry feet, use the footbridge.

Carry on up towards Povey Farm between the high hedges. The track bends left and then right. As it bends next left in sight of the farm, turn sharp right through the gateway (beware, this turn is unmarked) keeping to the left edge of the field with lovely views across the valley. Just after the path bends left down the hill, it turns diagonally across the field and straight into the wood at the bottom. Just a little further down you meet a fence and stile with stepping stones over the stream to your left. Cross these stones up the track towards the farm yard. At the top of the track turn right signposted 'Sheffield Country Walk to Ford'.

The tricky navigation is now over. Congratulations if you are still on the route: if you aren't, I've no idea where you are either!

You can now relax as you walk along the road past Birleyhay to Ford, the Bridge Inn, toilets and a picnic area- an excellent resting spot for all tastes.

Further Information on this Walk

Beauchief Abbey:
http://beauchiefabbey.org.uk/

Francis Leggat Chantry:
http://www.derbyshireuk.net/chantry.html

SECTION 6: FORD TO HALFWAY

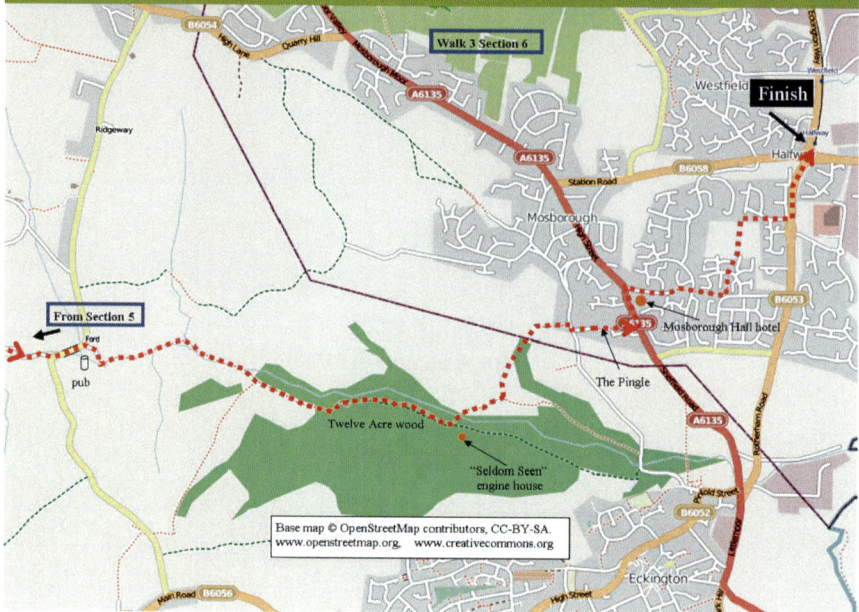

Base map © OpenStreetMap contributors, CC-BY-SA.
www.openstreetmap.org.   www.creativecommons.org

Directions

Suitably refreshed, take the path past the pub and the right hand side of the fishing pond along the very popular track across a couple of footbridges, ignoring the track up to the left just past a section of large black service pipe on your left. After just under 1km, you reach the next old fishing pond on your left. Just past the pond take the white footbridge to your right over the stream up to the edge of the field and then along into Twelve Acre wood.

At the other end of the wood (after about 1km) you reach a wide crossroads, usually with piles of felled timber stacked around. If you still have any energy left at this point, just off our intended route, about 100 metres ahead and to the right,

The Section

**Distance:
3.5 miles/
5 km**

**Time:
Allow 1½
hrs**

hidden in the trees there is the strangely named 'Seldom Seen' 19th Century engine house, the remains of the Plumbley colliery.

If you just need to get to the tram stop, at this wide crossroads turn left over a footbridge and head diagonally right onto an unusual hedged track between the fields. Keeping on this track, after about a further 200 metres, as the track bends to the right, turn left up a much smaller, currently unmarked track, and head up the left edge of a field towards the left hand edge of Ladybank Wood.

Follow up to the top of the field and over the stile. Turn right up to the gate and then left along the top of the field keeping the edge of the wood just on your right. Go over another stile in the top corner of the field. Now, head up across this next, often overgrown, field aiming for the top far right hand corner and a stone stile between two buildings. (You won't see this stile until you reach the end of the hedge.) Cross this stile and carry on between the buildings until you reach the road.

... really atmospheric!

...the old Mosborough Hall Hotel

Turn right and then left in front of the cottages along a peculiarly atmospheric, high stone-walled path in an area known locally as The Pingle.

At the end of this path, turn left at the road and take the next right into Hollow Lane and past the old Mosborough Hall Hotel on the right. Continue along the path ahead, across the next road, Auckland Way, and down to the next road, which is actually the re-commencement of Hollow Lane.

Here, take the footpath between the houses on your immediate left, across the next road and down the path opposite. You come out at the bottom corner of a playing field. Continue straight ahead in the same direction and at the end, turn right down the footpath onto School Avenue and a little further down still, onto the main road. Opposite is a large supermarket if any sustenance is required.

Turn left here, which takes you down to the roundabout and the welcome sight of the Halfway tram stop with the final river valley of the Rother out of sight down to the right.

Further Information on this Walk

Graves Park:
http://www.gravesparksheffield.info/?page_id=34

The Engine House:
http://www.derbyshire.gov.uk/leisure/countryside/countryside_sites/wildlife_amenity/engine_house/default.asp

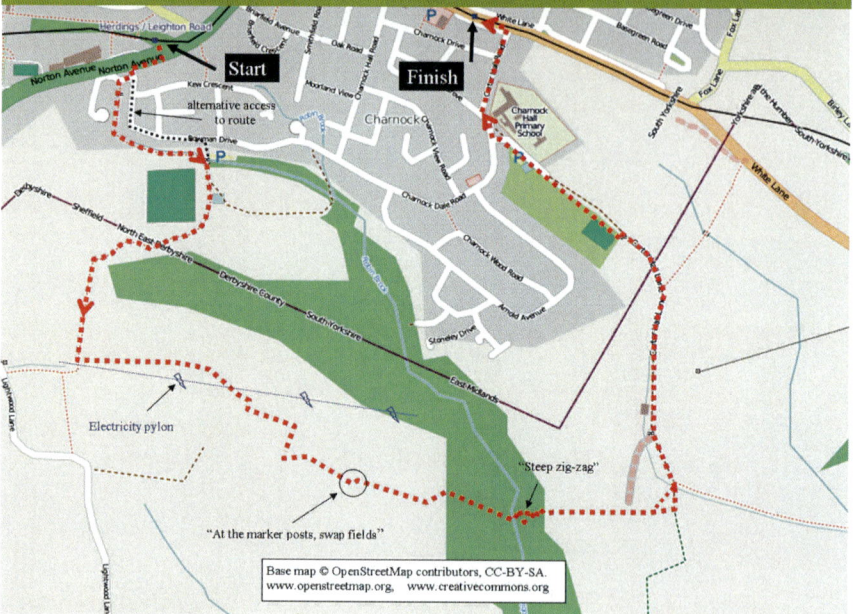

WALK FOUR

HERDINGS & LEIGHTON ROAD TO WHITE LANE

Description

Although the two tram stops are a mere 10 minutes walk apart by road, this gentle walk takes you across the old aerodrome, through farmland and woods, round a lovely little section of countryside across the Yorkshire-Derbyshire boundary and back. There is just one short steep climb.

Distance:
3 miles/
5 km

Time:
Allow 1½ hrs

Start: Herdings & Leighton Road Tram Stop

Finish: White Lane Tram Stop

41

Directions

Leave the tram stop and cross the dual carriageway. Turn left up Bowman Drive and immediately right onto Bowman Close. In 15 metres turn left down the signposted path between the houses. A word of warning: don't try this section in high summer wearing shorts. It contains giant nettles. If it's too overgrown, take the alternative access along Bowman Drive (see map).

Having battled the 50 or so metres to the end, you will see the large concrete boundary wall of the old Norton aerodrome (in fact, actually used as a barrage balloon station during the war). Turn left along the backs of the houses with the concrete wall of the aerodrome on your right. Soon you meet a track going at right angles with a metal gate on your left. Turn right up this track with a field on your left and football pitches up to your right through the trees.

Carry on along the track taking the right fork round the edge of the football field. You walk past an old skateboarding area and, keeping to the right hand side, go past (or over if you like) a small hump in the path. Just past here it's better to drop down left onto a wider, easier path going in the same direction up through the trees. You also pass some unfriendly 'Private land except ...' signs. Ignoring these, carry on past an old bunker on our right and, just after you leave the tree cover, turn left along the track between the grazing fields. You are now in Derbyshire.

Go through the hedge, along the right hand edge of the next field and turn left just before the stile along the edge of the same field following the line of the electricity pylons. Continue along the path as it passes over a stile and then under the cables to the edge of the field and onto the track.

Turn right at the track and then in 20 metres turn left over a stile along the left hand edge of the field to the far end. Don't be tempted to go through onto the next field ahead but continue round to the right in this field, past a young oak tree, to the path marker post 20 metres further on (this marker is often well-hidden in the undergrowth). Turn left and along the right hand edge of the field down to a sunken track.

Turn left up this track and follow it up and just over the brow and then, veering slightly to the left at the marker posts, swap fields keeping in the same direction and now keep the hedge on your right as you descend along the edge of the field The path enters the wood just past where, from a distance, it seems to be.

Follow the path all the way down the wood to the stream. Turn right immediately over the stream for 20 metres up to a junction and then straight on up via the steps in front which zigzag up the short but very steep hill between the holly bushes. As you reach the stile at the top, pause for breath and cross the field to the stile ahead. At the other end of the field, climb the next stile (or walk round, if the fencing is still missing).

Private land except ...

Carry on ahead beyond the next field and then either:
(a) head down diagonally left through the next field using the unmarked metal gate just behind the tree. Go down and through the metal gate in the bottom corner of the field or
(b) carry on along the top of and then left down the end of the field. Just after where (a) and (b) meet again, at the bottom gate, climb over a stile and on your left in 10 metres notice the small pond.

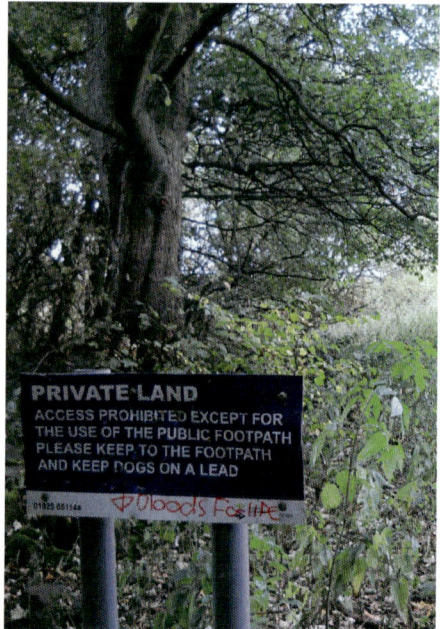

Carry straight on up the hill to the next gate and stone stile as you then enter a leafy track. Turn up to the right as you meet the track from the farm and carry on up past Carter Lodge.

43

… and then you enter a leafy track

To relieve the tedium of the track, as you walk up back into Yorkshire turn off left onto the playing field and stroll up, parallel with the lane, to the top. At the top, turn right down Carterhall Road past Charnock School to White Lane at the bottom. Turn left to catch the tram at White Lane stop.

Further Information on this Walk

Norton Aerodrome:

https://www.sheffield.gov.uk/planning-and-city-development/regeneration/neighbourhood-regeneration/your-neighbourhood/norton/norton-aerodrome.html

WALK FIVE

HALFWAY TO MEADOWHALL

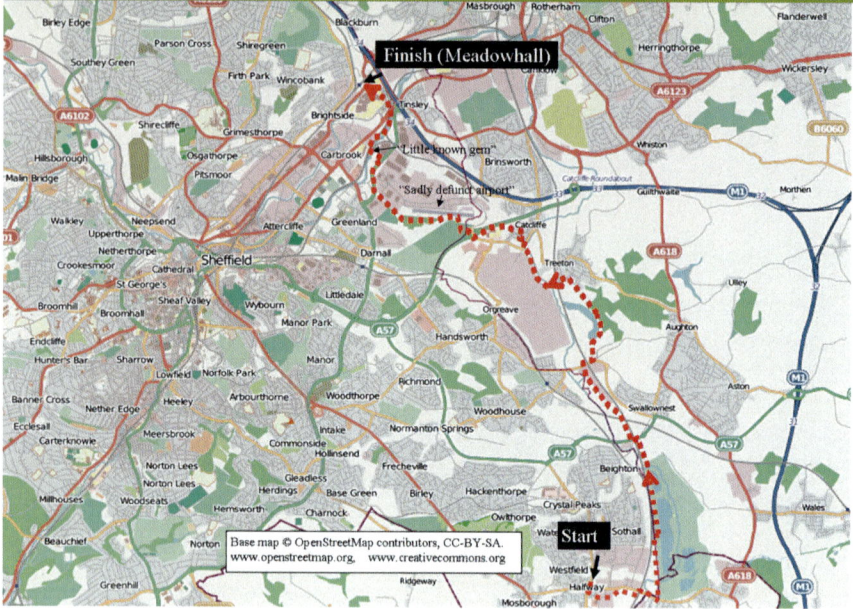

Description

Without doubt this walk is varied. There are some less than scenic sections coupled with bits of road walking. However, these are compensated for by the relatively easy walking, pleasant country parks and surprising oases found along the way.

Distance:
12 miles/
19 km

Time:
Allow 4-5 hrs

Start: Halfway Tram Stop

Finish: Meadowhall Tram Stop

Directions

*(Note: at the time of writing, work has just started on a new bridleway from Halfway tram stop directly to Killamarsh at the point * in the text below, but until it is completed, please follow the guidance below to get there without risking life and limb on the main road.)*

Leave the tram stop towards the roundabout. Go across the roundabout up the road towards Eckington and Staveley for about 30 metres. Then turn left down the path between the houses, across a road and continue down, passing an interesting faces sculpture on your left. The path comes out to a road with factories on either side.

Continue down along the road until at the end you veer slightly left onto a narrow, high-hedged path which leads between a factory and a skip yard. This leads out nearly to the main road. Here, you should return to the busy main road and continue right over the next bridge. Don't go on to the main road but instead, turn right over some rubble and into a wide, old and untidy area of land. *(Please note, that until the new bridleway is complete, this is still technically private land, although clearly not actively used, apart from by the locals.)* Turn sharp left again into the trees along a somewhat rubbish strewn and heavily rutted track.

Keep in the same direction, ignoring turnings first on the left and then on the right. Eventually you reach the end at a T-junction. Turn left here, then quickly right before the bridge, to climb the steps back up to the road.

Turn right over the railway bridge. Walk on over the railway and river. Just before you enter Killamarsh * under the next bridge, take the steps/ramp on the right hand side up to the track and turn left back over the bridge.. Carry on along this trail, which is now part of the Trans-Pennine Trail Route 67, for about 1.5km, ignoring a couple of turning options until you eventually reach a gate and stile with a path running at right angles across, with Trans-Pennine Trail direction signs. Turn right here, down under a bridge and into Rother

Trans-Pennine Trail Route 67

Valley Country Park with the clubhouse and slipway directly over the lake (initially obscured by trees).

Turn left along the edge of the lake and stroll down past both lakes into the bottom corner of the park. Take the path up to the left, about 50 metres before the fence and gate at the bottom end of the lake.

Go down the steps but don't carry on over the bridge in front. Instead, turn right over the old stone railway-style footbridge over the river. Go over the bridge, carry straight on along the side of the railway. Eventually you approach the new road bridge ahead. Here you must make a detour to get over to the other side of the railway by first turning right and climbing up to the road.

Then turn left across the bridge, left again down the side road, left again towards the railway and then left again through the stile. Finally you are now on the other side of the railway. Carry on, under the new road bridge you have just walked across, into Woodhouse Washlands Nature Reserve. Go straight on along the path under a red brick railway viaduct.

Treeton Dyke

The path then starts to bend away from the embankment on your right with the red brick viaduct now up on your left. Just before you reach the gate and stile ahead, follow the track round to the right and over the wooden bridge.

Then it's straight ahead along the right edge of the reserve with the factories just over the hedges to your right. (If you wish, you could take the parallel route 100 metres over to the left along the immediate bank of the Rother and look for the kingfishers). In either case, at the end of the reserve, pass a small winding gear sculpture and take the track to the right through a wooden swing gate and between the factories out to the busy main road.

Cross over to the other side and turn right. Just down in the dip, turn left into Falconer Lane past the row of terraced houses and go straight ahead through the gate towards Treeton Dyke. Carry on, ignoring a couple of left turns, along the right hand side of the lake into the edge of the curiously named Hail Mary wood. Eventually, as the track turns up to the right, turn left over a raised walkway with metal railings along the edge of the lake. Just over the walkway, the path meets a track to the sailing club house.

48

Go straight across this track and up the hill through two "boulder" barriers. At the second one, turn immediately left along the side of the hedge (don't carry on up to the top of the hill). Keeping the field below tight on your left, the path drops between hedges, through a metal stile and straight on past a playground on your left to the road. Turn left down Washfield Lane past the cricket club and into Hemingway Close. Carry straight on over the railway footbridge and then straight ahead through the barrier into the new Waverley development. *(Note: At the time of writing, this area is still a work in progress but walkers are allowed as long as we stick to the rules posted on the notices).*

Go ahead and over the metal bridge in front, turning right to follow the river bank past an old dilapidated blue bridge. All this area, when finished, will be a world away from the notorious 1984 Orgreave conflict between the miners and the police which took place over on the far side.

The track is somewhat undefined here. However, continue along and, within a couple of hundred yards, you can drop down to the small track immediately beside the river.

Eventually the track splits. Take the right hand option at the side of the river. This quickly meets the road just ahead. Cross over and turn right and quickly left along Orgreave Road and left up California Drive. In 20 metres, turn right up the path between houses Nos. 34 and 35 (oddly, these houses are numbered consecutively). Turn left along the back onto Willan Drive.

Ignore the first turn left and at the next junction turn left and 10 metres before Woodland Close, turn right up the path between the new houses. At the road, turn right, then left up the next path past the back of the houses and out along the edge of the field.

Carry on straight up along the edge, right up to the top as you near the busy Sheffield Parkway on the right. Carry on straight ahead, directly under the advertising gantry ahead, with the stores on your left and the busy Parkway on your right.

... a little known gem

Go straight up the grassy bank ahead. Keep the office block on your left side and walk down the side of the slip-road that leads to the roundabout, turning right under the specially-built pedestrian underpass (immediately on the far side of the road bridge but not easy to spot from this direction) to the roundabout beyond. Take the signposted path on the other side of the roundabout up to the left.

As the path enters the trees, turn sharp right up the hill, veering left at the next fork. This leads to the perimeter fence of the now defunct airport, with fine views across to the old terminal buildings. Turn left along the track with the golf course on your immediate left. As you draw level with the tenth tee, the main path veers to the left. Ignore this, and turn off up to the right through the metal barriers onto the track which runs along side the airport fence.

As the track climbs up the hill take the right fork, keeping the runway in sight, to your right. It's worth a pause up here to admire the views. Carry on along the track as it turns left up to a cross roads.

Turn right here, still following the line of the runway and keeping the airport fence on your right. Ignore the turning to the left and eventually (after taking in excellent views towards central Sheffield) you'll drop down to the right hand corner of the cemetery ahead. Go through some more metal barriers and turn right down the narrow track at the side of the cemetery

Continue down to the bottom where the path finally comes out onto Shepcote Lane. (This track is little used, so in summer it might be overgrown for the last 50 metres or so.)

At Shepcote Lane, cross over and turn right for about 1 km passing one set of traffic lights and a road down to the left. Carry along the main road and as it descends, just past the next set of traffic lights, turn left into Lock House Walk towards the lock keepers houses. Keeping the houses on your left, veer right and then climb the canal footbridge, pausing to admire the rise of locks in both directions. This is yet another relatively little-known gem of a place in the most unexpected area of Sheffield.

Over the bridge, turn right along the canal towpath, passing several more locks along the way. Go under the next road bridge then, ignoring the first turn up to the left, carry on for 50 metres through the stile and turn left up to the footbridge over the tracks. You can catch the tram at this stop or continue the walk, heading towards, and through, the Meadowhall Shopping complex to the Interchange and Meadowhall Tram Stop.

Further Information on this Walk

The Transpennine Trail:
http://www.transpenninetrail.org.uk/

Orgreave 1984
http://news.bbc.co.uk/onthisday/hi/dates/stories/may/29/newsid_2494000/2494793.stm

Rotherham Unofficial - Treeton Dyke
http://www.rotherhamunofficial.co.uk/recreation/parks/woodlandsetc/treetondyke.html

Rotherham Unofficial - Nature Reserves
http://www.rotherhamunofficial.co.uk/recreation/parks/woodlandsetc/index.html

WALK SIX

HALFWAY TO WATERTHORPE VIA ROTHER VALLEY COUNTRY PARK

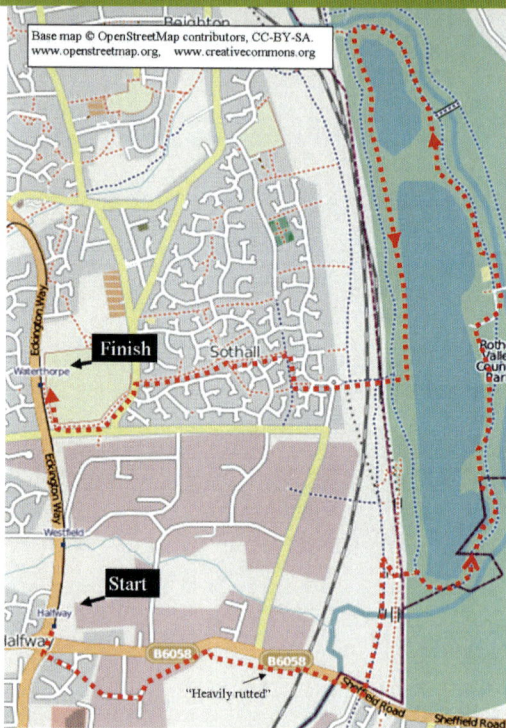

Base map © OpenStreetMap contributors, CC-BY-SA.
www.openstreetmap.org,   www.creativecommons.org

Description

Probably the gentlest suburban walk in the book. After the same start as Walk 5, it is a pleasant ramble via the varied delights of the country park.

Start: Halfway Tram Stop;

Finish: Waterthorpe Tram Stop

Distance:
4 miles/
6.5 km

Time:
Allow 1½ hrs

Directions

Leave the tram and head away towards the roundabout. Go across the roundabout up the road to Eckington only for about 20 metres. Then turn left down the path between the houses, across a road and continue down, passing an interesting faces sculpture on your left. The path comes out at a road with factories on either side.

Continue along the road until at the end, you veer slightly left onto a narrow, high-hedged path which leads between a factory and a skip yard. This leads out nearly to the main road. At the end, before the road, turn right over some rubble and into a wide, old and untidy area of land.

Turn sharp left again into the trees along a somewhat rubbish strewn and, in parts, heavily rutted track, keeping more or less in the same direction with the sound of the road nearby on the left. Eventually you reach the end at a T-junction. Turn left here, then quickly right before the bridge to climb the steps back up to the road.

Turn right over the railway bridge and ahead you can see another bridge just past the Derbyshire sign. Just as you approach the large Killamarsh sign at the bridge over the road, take the steps/ramp on the right hand side up onto the track and turn left back over the bridge.

Carry on along this track, crossing the River Rother after about 300 metres. Just a little further on take the track which bends back down to the right, turning left under a bridge out to the bottom edge of the cable-ski lake in the Rother Valley country park.

Turn right and skirt the lake all the way round to the gate. Turn right and then drop back down to the water's edge towards the sailing centre.

Just before you reach the centre you have to detour round the edge of the compound and come out near the playground.

The choice is now yours. You can idle away many hours watching, participating or just strolling round the visitor centre, over to the right.

When you are ready to carry on, head back to the edge of the lake and follow it round, continuing in an anti-clockwise direction. At the bottom of the first lake turn left along the bottom then head back left up the far side.

As you get about level with the sailing centre, now on the far side, you reach a clump of trees on your left. Just ahead, turn right up the track out of the park and under a bridge. Go over the railway bridge, straight on under the electricity cables past a gate and up to the roundabout.

Go straight across the roundabout and up the road opposite for about 40 metres. Take the footpath straight ahead at the side of the Mill Meadow Gardens road sign.

...interesting faces in the park

55

...and varied delights

Carry on to the footpath T- junction where you now turn right towards Beighton. Walk along this footpath between the houses and after about 150 metres, turn left at the next footpath junction (*before* you reach the road ahead).

This takes you up to, and directly across, a road onto another path. Follow this as it opens out with a playground on your right. Carry on up past the playground, more or less straight up in the same direction, until you reach the main road. Cross over the road, turn left and take the path right round the edge Westfield school playing fields to come out at Waterthorpe tram stop.

Further Information on this Walk

Rother Valley Country Park:

http://www.rothervalleycountrypark.co.uk/

WALK SEVEN
MEADOWHALL TO MIDDLEWOOD

Base map © OpenStreetMap contributors, CC-BY-SA.
www.openstreetmap.org,   www.creativecommons.org

Description

A relatively gentle walk with a few longer climbs along mainly well defined paths. However, probably best attempted either side of high summer because of a few, short overgrown stretches. You travel through woods, parks and farms with views appearing at unexpected moments.   Even the urban areas are crossed using surprisingly pleasant tracks.

Start: Meadowhall Interchange Tram Stop

Finish: Middlewood Tram Stop

Distance:
7 miles/
11 km

Time:
Allow 3-3½ hrs

57

Directions

Leave the tram stop and, instead of heading with the crowd for the Meadowhall centre, head the other way towards Platform 4. Go over the bridge and turn right up the steps and along the path out of the station, turning right along Tyler Road.

Continue along the road for about 1km, through one set of lights, past the primitive Methodist chapel on your left and the gasometers to your right. At the junction at the bottom of the hill, go straight across, along Ecclesfield Road. Just past the houses on the left, take the footpath signposted on the left, up the hill with the playground on your right. Just before the path enters the trees at the top, turn diagonally right across the grass and along the track into Woolley Wood. Follow the main path through these woods as it bends and twists for nearly 2km, ignoring the numerous other paths which join and cross. The path runs more or less parallel with the road which you see or hear down to your right all the way along. On the way you'll pass through several low wooden barriers

Near the end, you'll see a fork down to the road and a metal anti-bike barrier. Ignore this, and carry on a little further on the main path where it soon opens out about 20 ft above Ecclesfield Road with fleeting views across the valley to the 18th Century Thundercliffe Grange (now a co-housing community) nestling in the trees, and the M1 sweeping across into the distance. Continue a little further on and down to the end of the path, through the gate and turn left along Ecclesfield Road. Go past the bottom of Bellhouse Road, cross over and take the footpath opposite, down into the trees and away from the road.

This drops down to run alongside a stream and, a little further beyond, the railway. Continue along this path ignoring a footbridge coming over the stream on your right and the track up to the left but, instead carry on along the side of the stream, past another small bridge and, eventually, a small weir (partly hidden amongst the bushes) Just after here, the track bends again to meet the road. Turn

...the church beyond the bowling green

right along the road, carrying straight on past the Civil Service sports ground on your left to the junction. Turn right onto The Common, past the police station and then, 100 metres further on, turn left into the park opposite the supermarket. Go over the little footbridge and then turn right up through the avenue of trees. Just before the tennis courts, turn left passing the playground on your left and a pleasant view of St Mary's church beyond the bowling-green to your right.

As the path comes to a grassy bank in front, turn left over a stone flagged bridge and either climb the old authentic cobbled path up between the houses to the road or keep ahead along the lower path. In either case, at the road, turn right down the hill to the junction with the ancient St Mary's church opposite.

Turn left at this junction, then right up the lane, up the side of the church yard, noting the stocks which are well used for the obligatory wedding photo. Also in the church grounds is the vault of Reverend (Doctor) Scott in whose arms Nelson died at the battle of Trafalgar. On your left you pass the Gatty (an eminent previous vicar) Memorial

...the side of the Gatty Memorial Building

building (1904). On your right is the John Hawthorn Memorial gateway into the church yard (1904).

Take the footpath to the left up the side of the Gatty Memorial building past the cemetery on your right. Carry on past the end of the cemetery wall up on your right, keeping to the top edge of the *next* field. It veers right, up past a horse shelter, to the top corner and over a stile. Go along the ridge in the next field and then, halfway along, head diagonally down to the far bottom left hand corner. You probably can't see it for the bushes, but be assured, there is a stile behind there. Go over the stile and then straight across the cultivated field to the path between the houses and out onto the road.

Turn right along 'The Wheel' and after 200 metres turn left up the path along the edge of a small wood out into a field. Carry on along the left edge, veering right and then left again until it drops down to the left to a very small stream. Cross the stream and immediately turn sharp right as the path climbs up the field along the edge of the stream.

Ignoring the entrance to the next field on the right, head towards the right hand end of the houses ahead, taking the

path in the bushes between the hedges up a few steps to the road. Turn left, passing Yewlands Technical College on your right.

... passing
Birley Hall on
your left

At the junction of Creswick Lane and Yew Lane, turn right up the wide foot/cycle path between the schools, straight up the hill to a small side road. Turn right, then quickly left up the steps to the busy Halifax Road. Go straight across and up the path on the other side between the houses with Holme Lane farm over to your right behind the fence and hedges. If you're doing this walk in high summer, then at this point find yourself a good-sized stick.

The path drops down some steps and then up the other side towards the back of the houses at the the top of the road. This path can be overgrown, hence the stick (sometimes the locals choose to walk up the field parallel to the path). At the top, turn left, recover from the nettling if necessary and then walk along for about 200 metres.

Turn right up the footpath towards Shaw Hill Farm, turning left as directed immediately in front of the farm along the

... diagonally down the track

edge of the garden and, keeping the fence immediately on your right until it ends, climb a short way to the crest of the hill through two stone gate posts. Pause here to enjoy the pleasant and somewhat unexpected views.

Carry on straight ahead, down between two stone walls along the back of some gardens (still got the stick?), down the stone steps to a lane and veer right out to the road, Turn left along and up Edge Lane, passing Birley House on your right and Birley Hall on your left.

Just over the brow of the hill take the footpath signposted to the left through the bushes out to the top of the ridge. You're now standing (or you might want to sit and rest awhile) on Birley Edge. An excellent view from here.

Don't continue along the track to the left along the top. The plan is to head diagonally down to the left to the cottages you can see below you in the valley. So turn initially right, then quickly diagonally left down the track heading amongst the bracken down the hill to the farms. Again, if you are here in high summer, the going gets a little overgrown (stick or no stick). Turn right down any of the smaller tracks to the path along the bottom turning left to join up further on. At the bottom of the hill, turn right over a wall, along the right hand side of a field and then very tightly up against the right edge of the right hand cottage out to the road.

Turn left down the lane for 50 metres and then right over a stile and up the right edge of the field. Go over the stile, turning right towards the farm. Be aware, it's always very churned up and muddy around here. Go through the stone gate posts then immediately left, nearly back on yourself down the left edge of the field towards the pylon with views on your left over Hillsborough and back to the city centre.

At the edge of the field, don't go over the stile, but turn right along the edge of the field you are in, over a wooden stile onto a track between the hedges into the woods with the power lines on your left. The path veers left underneath a pylon. Just past this, you cross a broken down wall and fence into the wood.

Take no more than about five steps away from this wall and then take the small track to the left, keeping the boundary wall in sight on your left. After about 400 metres (your trusty stick might get a bit of use), the track meets a wider one. Turn left down the hill to cross the spooky railway at Rocher Bridge.

Carry on, with the factory fence immediately on your left down the stepped path to a service road. Turn right for 100 metres towards the factory, then left at the small car park, around the side of the factory along the side of the river. Turn left over the river at the footbridge and then left again along the other bank, past a weir (where the industrial aroma of the river can be enjoyed).

As you reach a small, brilliant orange outfall opposite, the path turns right away from the river up to the road opposite Stockarth Lane. Bid a fond farewell to your stick and turn left, past the park for about a kilometre or so back to Middlewood tram stop.

Further Information on this Walk

St Mary's Parish Church, Ecclesfield:
http://www.stmarysecclesfield.com/index.html

Fuelling a Revolution - Woolley Wood:
http://www.heritagewoodsonline.co.uk/map/035/035.htm

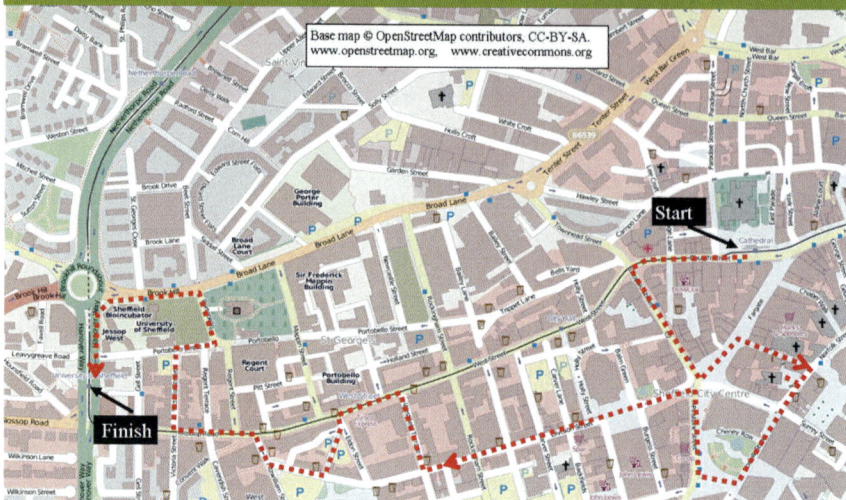

WALK EIGHT
CATHEDRAL TO UNIVERSITY

Description

This is just a bit of light hearted fun, a meander round the city centre, picking out the bits and pieces that are not usually noticed during the rush of daily life. It's not intended to be a detailed historical or architectural tour, but perhaps an excuse to avoid the shopping. The walk is paved all the way and is suitable for all.

Kids should enjoy the 'I-Spy' element, trying to see how many of the photos, A to U, they can find en-route, located in the text at points 1 to 21.

Start: Cathedral Tram Stop

Finish: University Tram Stop

Distance:
1½ miles/ 2.5km

Time:
Allow a leisurely hour

Directions

Walk up Church Street away from the tram stop and the cathedral. On the left is the Cutlers Hall. High up on the frontage are the coats of arms with elephant heads sporting large tusks, a symbol of the ivory handles used by the cutlers in an earlier age (1).

Just up from the Cutlers Hall is the old Midland Bank. Looking through the left hand gateway, you can see a turntable set into the far end of the driveway. This was provided to allow vehicles to be turned in the confined space and thus avoid having to reverse, presumably for security reasons.

Carry on up Church Street to Vicar Lane on the right. The building on the opposite corner has a sober faced judge carved over the doorway, with several typically shaped gargoyles nearby and a sundial ('*Tempus Fugit*') set in the wall to the left (2).

Go past Orchard Lane and turn left into Leopold Street, passing the old Central Schools building over the road on the right. This area is now a trendy restaurant and apartment complex At the other end of the building, on the corner, is a carving denoting Sheffield School Board with, above, the carved head of what is possibly a benefactor (3).

Head along Leopold Street towards the Town Hall and stop at the top of Fargate.

On your right, on the corner of Leopold Street and Barker's Pool is H L Browns. Above the ground floor windows is the locally famous One o'clock time signal (4), which used to be just across the road before the redevelopment of Orchard Square. Higher up on the same building is the plaque 'Cabinet Makers to HRH Prince of Wales', a reference to the previous occupants, Wilson Peck (5).

Turn left down Fargate, noting all the little stone carved figures on the buildings to the right.

I

L

J

M

K

N

O

P

Q

R

69

On the corner of Norfolk Row, above and to the right of the doorway to Carmel House, you can test your bible knowledge. The six days of the Creation are portrayed on the building from left to right (6).

Turn round and face W H Smiths. Again, high up on the frontage you can see the carved heads of pigs and boars. This building used to house Davy's, originally a pork butchers – hence the carvings (7).

Turn round again and wander down Norfolk Row past the birthplace of Sheffield United, noting the plaque (8), with St Marie's Catholic Cathedral on the left. At the end, note the religious carving in the wall (9).

Turn right up Norfolk Street for about 20 metres and then right again into the Upper Chapel courtyard. Here is another sundial ('Number only the sunny hours') and various sculptures in a lovely little haven of peace (10).

Leave the courtyard by the same gate and turn right. The first doorway you pass has the curious inscription above the doorway 'Jeffie Bainbridge's Children's Shelter' (11).

Carry on up and across Surrey Street along the back of the old Town Hall. The second doorway along on the right is inscribed 'Disinfectants', clearly a reflection of the sanitation and medical standards at the turn of the century (12).

Carry on past the back of the old Town Hall and into the Peace Garden area. Here, you should be able to achieve three objectives:

> One: spot the Bochum bell in the far top corner, which is a gift to us from our twin city in Germany (13).

> Two: find the old official standard measurements on the wall on Cheney Row, at the side of the Town Hall (14).

> Three: resist the temptation to run the fountain gauntlet.

After drying out if you failed objective three, turn right at the top of the Peace Gardens along Pinstone Street to the front of the Town Hall. Passing along the front, notice the frieze depicting the variety of manual skills for which Sheffield is historically renowned (15).

At the far corner you'll find Sheffield's only surviving traditional police box. Turn left up into Barker's Pool past Pool Square and the site of the old small reservoir that was used to periodically sluice the city centre gutters in the days before sewers.

Continue up to the war memorial flag pole and face the City Hall. On December 12th 1940, a German bomb landed where you are now standing, destroying a water tank and showering the surrounding area with shrapnel. The repaired damage marks can clearly be seen on the columns of the City Hall.

Carry on up Division Street, past the City Hall. The first building on Division Street on the right was the old Sheffield Water Works Company offices – see the clue on the facade. Walk on up along Division Street past the old Central Fire Station now a bar with apartments above (16).

As you stroll along, the route passes several small alleys on both sides. Along these you catch glimpses of the remnants of 'little mesters', a term generally used to describe self employed cutlery or small tool craftsmen. Their factories and workshops once filled most of this area. Several of the larger ones are still standing and some have been converted into trendy apartments.

Turn right up Westfield Terrace with the Zion Mount chapel frontage on the left (17). This served also as the entrance to the outpatients department to the Royal Hospital which occupied most of the block behind. Further up on the right is a pleasant little trio of doorways, with their elegance now somewhat faded (18).

At the junction with West Street, look to the right at Hutton's Building and just a little further on, Tiger Works, with appropriate carvings just above the doorway. Turn left along West Street past the tram stop and turn left into Eldon Street.

Turn immediately diagonally right, across Eldon Street and down the foot/cycle path past the 'J Webb Patent Sewer Gas Destructor' lamp post and the small car park on the right. This leads to the Wharncliffe Fire Clay Works (1888) on your left. It is more ornate than the surrounding buildings (19).

Turn right along Devonshire Street and right at the end, back up to West Street. Turn left along West Street, past Convent Walk, the strangely proportioned bank and the old Glossop Road Baths, all on the left.

Turn right up Victoria Street to the Church of the Nazerene on the left. The church boasts both a tower and a spire, which some consider gives the building a doll's house appearance, cute but lacking a sense of proportion.

At the junction with the old Jessops Hospital, and another of J Webbs Patent Sewer Gas Destructors (20), turn right and then left along the side of the old hospital boundary. Cross over, past the entrance to the churchyard and head to the corner and the junction with Broad Lane. Just over the wall in the churchyard is a raised tombstone with an unusual, musically engraved epitaph (21).

Turn left up Broad Lane to the roundabout, (the tram line runs under the roundabout at this point) and then left again, down to the University Tram Stop; note the premises of the world famous Henderson's Relish on the left.

Further Information on this Walk

Sheffield City Centre:
http://en.wikipedia.org/wiki/Sheffield_City_Centre

Sheffield Town Hall:
https://www.sheffield.gov.uk/out--about/tourist-information/town-hall.html

Sheffield Blitz:
https://www.sheffield.gov.uk/libraries/archives-and-local-studies/publications/blitz.html

Sheffield's Sewer Gas Destructor Lamps:
http://en.wikipedia.org/wiki/Sewer_gas_destructor_lamp

WALK NINE

SHALESMOOR TO HILLSBOROUGH PARK

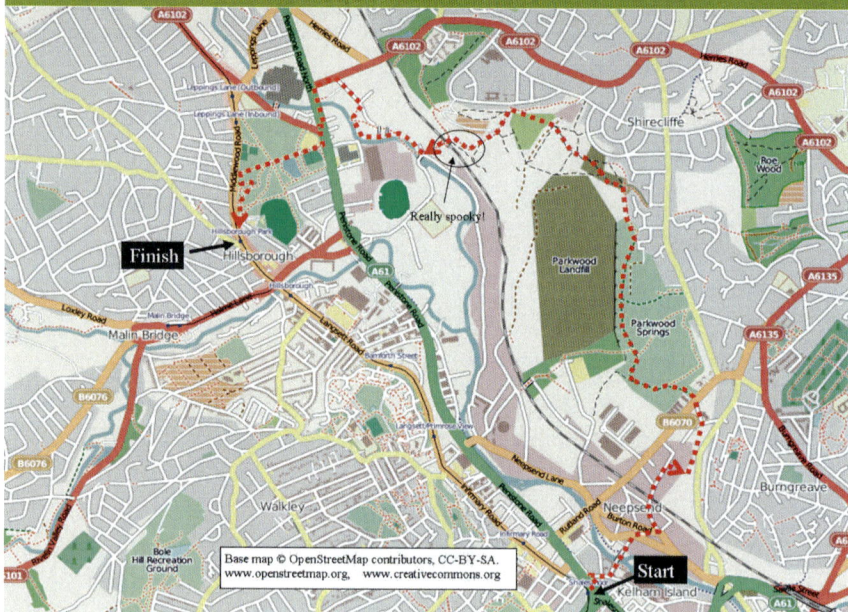

Description

Don't do this walk alone! I'm not trying to scare you. It's nothing to do with personal security and most of the walk is fine. There are some grim, rubbish-strewn sections but they are worth it. The views are tremendous but the highlight (at least for me) is Ward's End cemetery. Even in broad daylight in the middle of summer it's really, really spooky. You have been warned!

Start: Shalesmoor Tram Stop

Finish: Hillsborough Park Tram Stop

Distance:
4 miles/
6.5 km

Time:
Allow 2½ hrs

75

Directions

Leave the tram stop and cross over the main road towards the Globe Works on your left, which was damaged by a bomb planted in 1843 during the infamous 'Sheffield Outrages', a long and bitter dispute between the emerging unions and the cutlery factory owners. Turn right along Green Lane.

Around here is another area of Sheffield rich in our industrial heritage. Luckily, many of the old cutlery and tool factories and buildings are being retained and renovated as desirable apartment blocks.

Walk along Green Lane and take the second left along Ball Street (currently there is no street sign) where you see the 'Alfred Beckett' sign up on the wall. Walk on to the bridge and admire the river frontages of the buildings to either side, with the weir to the right. The explanation of Alfred Beckett's role in the life of Sheffield is on the wall behind you. Not quite the left bank of the Seine but pleasing in its own way.

Go across Mowbray Street then diagonally to the right along Neepsend Lane (again, currently no street sign). Turn left along Harvest Lane (guess what? – currently no street

The Alfred Beckett works

sign) and veer right up towards and then under the railway bridge (probably one of the lowest height clearances in the whole of Sheffield) up Woodside Lane.

Carry on straight up for about 100 metres and turn right along an unmarked path for 30 metres between a building and a storage yard, then out through the trees to a grassy area with the Woodside housing estate in front. As you meet the path turn left, up between the trees and follow it, more or less straight up to the road, passing the old site of the world famous Stanley Tools factory, makers of the Stanley Knife and much else.

Go straight across and up Wood Fold (you've guessed it – currently no street name) noting the old stone house halfway up on the right. Cross Rutland Road and go straight up the public bridle-way into Parkwood Springs opposite. The path heads to the top of the hill veering to the left on the way up. Magnificent views over Sheffield begin to emerge. As the path keeps climbing further up, more views appear out to the moors and then, quite suddenly and in total contrast, the ski village appears over the horizon immediately in front.

Turn up to the right and, with the fence immediately on the left, turn left up the smaller track and pass under the actual ski lift cable, Don't veer left here, but go straight on up the hill along a track marked either side with stone kerbs as the views get more stunning with every step. Near the top, turn left up to the summit and viewing point (sadly, a little worse for wear).

Carry on along the path and in 20 metres are the remains of a WW II defence emplacement overlooking the site of many steelworks and utilities that used to be in the valley below, demonstrating the strategic importance of this hilltop.

Views to the right now begin to appear over the playing fields and also down to the immediate left, dominated by the landfill site which, thankfully, is being reinstated. Carry on along the undulating path through a metal 'anti-bike' stile, keeping the housing close on the right.

The Walled Garden … equally pleasing

Ignore the first path to the right leading out onto the road. Instead, veer slightly left and continue through more metal stiles along the narrow track between the backs of the houses and the boundary fence of the landfill site. Eventually the track breaks out from the houses as the fence turns away to the left. Carry on straight ahead and follow the main path across the open scrubland as it begins to descend behind some more houses.

Take the track down past the left hand side of the hillock in front and straight across the next junction at the bottom, passing the recycling site away at a distance on your right. Follow the track round to the right far corner of the field, through a metal gate and then turn immediately left down the hill through some old metal barriers..

Carry on, essentially straight down the hill, past the often fly-tipped entrance to the allotments on your right, taking the right fork near the bottom to meet the fenced railway cutting in front. You have now reached Wards End cemetery, with headstones everywhere in the under-growth.

Carry on along the path for a short way and through the gap in the fence to the bridge over the railway. At the far end of the bridge, look over the railings ahead. You see a path through the trees and graveyard going directly down the hill. When you've plucked up enough courage, head on down it.

... really, really spooky"

This must be the spookiest place in Sheffield, particularly in summer. You are surrounded by a forest of graves at all angles, all overgrown and competing with the trees for the available ground space. It's dark and, to add to the atmosphere, a sickly sweet aroma occasionally fills the air. (In fact, it's from the sweet factory nearby).

This cemetery was used for burying some of the military personnel based at the old Hillsborough Barracks, a short distance across the valley. One Lieutenant George Lambert lies here. He was awarded the Victoria Cross during the Indian Mutiny in 1857. Also resting here are many of the 240 victims of the Sheffield Flood of 1864. The cemetery was finally closed in 1988.

Carry on, thankfully into daylight, down the steps and turn right before the bridge along the river bank with the car breaker's yard up to the right. The path leads under two bridges which span the river Eventually, as the aromas from the factory come and go, the path turns sharply right away from the river up a narrow fenced track to the road. Turn left to the end and left again down Herries Road towards Hillsborough football ground.

At the main road, turn left over the bridge, noting Ward's End Steel Works sign set in the wall. Just before you reach Hillsborough Leisure centre on your left, cross over at the junction and go into the park through the main gates opposite. Carry on up the main path with the pond on your left and further up to the playground on your right.

About 50 metres before you reach the gates at the top, turn left along the side of the tall hedge and then right to the Walled Garden, if open. (If closed, carry on past the rear of the library building and then head diagonally right up to the park exit.)

Part of this garden was set up as a memorial to the 96 Liverpool fans who died in the Hillsborough tragedy of 1989 – hence the inscription over the gates. It is a beautiful oasis of tranquillity.

Continue round the corner into the walled garden, which is equally pleasing. Exit the walled garden through the doorway towards the library on your left. Head across the park to the far right and the Hawksley Avenue exit and then down a few metres to Hillsborough Park Tram Stop.

Further Information on this Walk

The Sheffield Outrages:

https://www.sheffield.gov.uk/libraries/archives-and-local-studies/publications/sheffield-outrages.html

Wardsend Cemetery:

http://www.friendsofwardsendcemetery.btck.co.uk/

Friends of Parkwood Springs:

http://www.parkwood-springs.btck.co.uk/

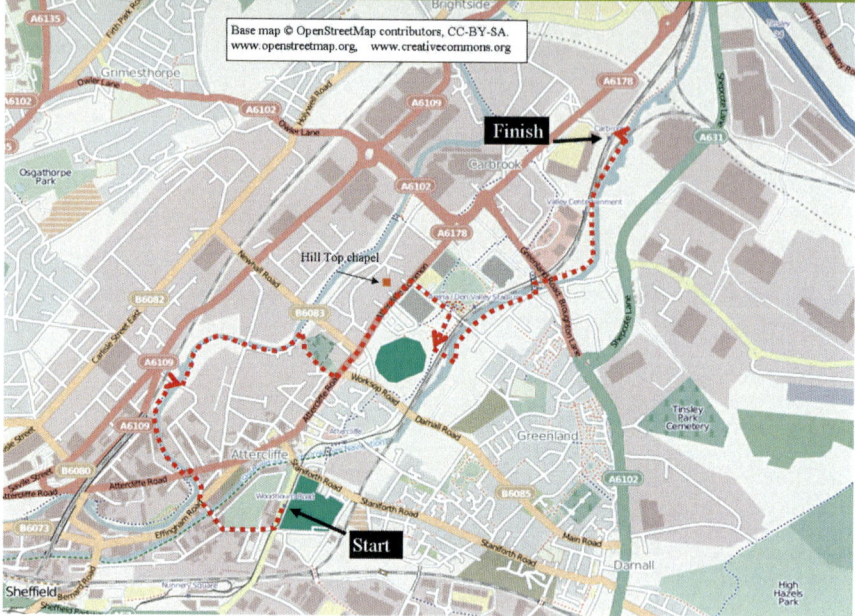

WALK TEN
WOODBOURN ROAD TO CARBROOK

Description

After an inauspicious first 200 yards, the walk increases in interest and surroundings the further you get. It contrasts old and new, river and canal, industry and leisure, with no hills to speak of!

Start: Woodbourn Road Tram Stop

Finish: Carbrook Tram Stop

Distance:
3.5 miles/
5.5 km

Time:
Allow 2 hrs

Directions

Leave the tram and walk along the platform towards the direction of the city centre. Turn right at the junction, down Worthing Road. Opposite the Woodbourn pub, turn right along Bacon Lane and as it narrows, go over the canal, which has now been here nearly 200 hundred years. (We come back to the canal later).

Go straight across Effingham Road and down Stoke Street opposite, noting the drunken bricklayer's handiwork on the building on the corner.

After 20 metres turn left along the side of the river to Attercliffe Road and then left over Washford Bridge. Although hard to believe now, this was once an idyllic spot in the country with the river teeming with fish; hence the name of the area, Salmon Pastures. At the far end of the bridge cross the main road and head along the side of the river on one of the sections of the Five Weirs Walk. There

The Five Weirs Walk

are many interesting facts about these sections of the river, which are well described on the information boards as you walk along.

The circular stone slab

Carry on this section past Royds Mills to the road, turn right over the bridge, noting the 'secret' little gap at the far end that leads down to the river, that my son spotted years ago. Turn left over the road and on to the next section of the Weirs walk past Sanderson's Weir.

Along here, on the right of the path you'll eventually see a circular stone slab, bearing a worn and indistinct inscription. You also may be able to see the associated art work on the opposite side of the river, now somewhat obscured by the foliage.

Carry on under the bridge to Stevenson Road, going straight across along another section. As the walk veers to the left, you see the slopes of Attercliffe cemetery ahead, just beyond the end of the works' fencing. Turn right here, to enter what is the rear of the cemetery. Either head straight up to visit the cemetery or follow the path inside the wall up to the right and then go left up the slope to the main entrance out onto Attercliffe Road.

...it has an almost rural atmosphere

Turn left here, down past Worksop Road, with the old baths on your right and the Adelphi Theatre down a road on your left. Cross the junction with Newhall Road, passing the main entrance to Don Valley stadium on your right.

Carry on past the Vestry Hall and the old Labour Exchange (a reminder of how many people used to live and work round here) until you reach the Hill Top chapel and graveyard. This is one of Sheffield's oldest surviving buildings (1629) and worth a look if the gates are open. Benjamin Huntsman, the inventor of crucible steel, lies buried in here.

Then return to the road, cross over and turn right up Coleridge Road, You now have the English Institute for Sport on your right and Ice Sheffield on your left. A further 200 metres along, at the main gate, turn left into the Don Valley Bowl, then right up the path which leads under the footbridge, then left up and back over it.

Once over the footbridge you reach what used to be a lovely rest area, but which is now rarely used. It had a sundial which few people understood. Currently, this area is sadly neglected. Go on and then after 50 metres take the path to the left (*not* the first one back down to the tram

86

stop) over two footbridges, first over the tram tracks and then over the canal. It's worth pausing on the second bridge to have a look round to appreciate the transformation in this area. Who would have thought that you would hear the sound of the Rolling Stones instead of the Brown Bailey steelworks? Some might say "What's the difference?"

Carrying on over the canal bridge, turn left down on to the tow path, under Pothouse Bridge with the Arena over the canal to the left. On reaching Broughton Lane, take the path before the bridge, up to the road and turn left across the bridge. Then walk right down the ramp onto the tow path on the other side of the canal. Walking along this section is almost rural in its atmosphere. Eventually you reach the first of the twelve Tinsley Locks, with the lock keepers' houses over to the right.

Just before the footbridge over the canal, turn left, away and down under the railway. Go over the footbridge over the tram track to Carbrook tram stop.

The 'Secret Little Gap', down to the river

Further Information on this Walk

The Five Weirs Walk:
http://www.fiveweirs.co.uk/

The Sheffield Canal:
http://en.wikipedia.org/wiki/Sheffield_Canal

WALK ELEVEN
MALIN BRIDGE, RIVELIN, LOXLEY

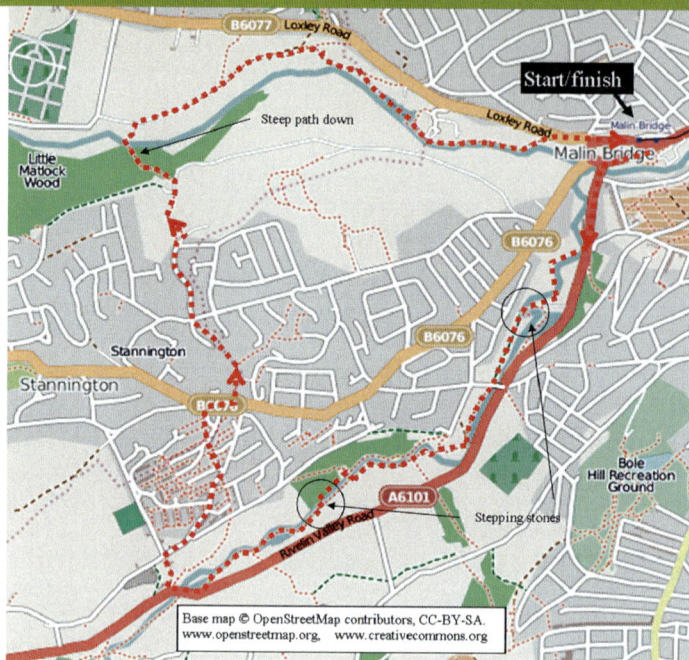

Base map © OpenStreetMap contributors, CC-BY-SA.
www.openstreetmap.org,   www.creativecommons.org

Description

This is a walk which takes you past evidence of our industrial heritage; the old water-driven mills with their dams and sluices that lined the river valleys of Sheffield. They were set in beautiful surroundings, as this walk proves. There is the option of crossing two sets of narrow stepping stones (easier alternatives are available) and a steep bit up to Stannington but nothing too strenuous.

Distance:
4 miles/
6.5 km

Time:
Allow 2 hrs

Start and Finish: Malin Bridge Tram Stop

89

Directions

Walk away from the tram terminus, taking the bottom road on the left towards Malin Bridge. Go past the 'Park and Ride' facility and La Plata Works on your left and turn left at the next road onto Rivelin Valley Road (A6101 to Glossop).

Cross the bridge noting the original bit of railings and old sluice gate on your left. Over the bridge parapet on the right you can see the confluence of the rivers Rivelin and Loxley. Carry on along the road and, just past the fire station, turn right over a stone bridge and then immediately left through very pleasant woods with the stream on your left.

The first of the evidence of our industrial heritage starts to appear. Cross the stream over a wooden bridge and turn right to keep the stream immediately on your right, past a weir and then over the stream again, this time on somewhat narrow stepping stones. Here, instead of falling off the stones, you can follow the river round, with the Rivelin pond appearing on your left. Then over the little bridge, up the path, out to the main road and first right again to meet up as below at the road.

...somewhat narrow stepping stones

The remains of an old waterwheel

The path climbs up to a road. Cross over the road and continue along the track with a paddling pool appearing over to the left beyond the weir. As you go beyond the paddling pool, the path goes through a gap in a wall. Turn left then right along the Rivelin Valley Trail past a playground on your right and then left over a bridge, turning right again. This is a very relaxing stretch of about 1km with the allotments to your left and the babbling stream to your right, on the far side of which are yet more remains of Sheffield's heritage. Look out for the mid-stream chair art work.

As you reach a stone footbridge, either carry straight on or, if you like a bit of adventure, turn right over it and then left along the other bank of the stream. You are passing the remains of another water mill on the right – well worth a quick investigation. You can still work out what was what.

Carry on to pass a weir on your left. Just past this, turn left over some narrow and occasionally wobbly stepping stones back across the stream and then turn right along the path. Here you join those who were less adventurous and took the easy route.

*Rivelin Glen
Mission*

There's plenty more evidence of industrial activity along here. At one point on your left you can see the remains of a water wheel's axle, lying amongst the debris of Holme Head wheel. At the fork in the path, just past the next weir, take the right option along the side of the stream, over a bridge, past another old dam on the left, and then another weir as the path opens out with a much larger dam to the right. Go up past the left hand side to the road.

Turn right over the bridge and at the far end, make a right angled turn, up the path that leads up towards the right hand edge of the cottages above. The path then turns sharp right in front of the cottage gate and becomes cobbled and a little steeper until it reaches the road, just past the currently boarded-up Rivelin Glen Mission on the left.

Turn right here as you reach the road (don't continue up Long Lane) and carry on up for about 300 metres as the road heads through the estate towards the tower blocks in the distance. Pass a post box on the left and 50 metres further on, at the bus stop, turn left up the steps between the houses of Liberty Place. Carry on across the road, right up to the top as the path veers a little from side to side.

At the top of Hall Park Mount you'll see the tower blocks across the road to the right and the Sportsman pub on the left. Turn right down Stannington Road and cross the road after 50 metres to turn left down the side of the tower block, leading to a narrow, grassy path that runs past the immediate edge of the blocks and out onto a usually very boggy field.

Head across this field to the left corner of the blocks of maisonettes you see ahead. The target is two old stone posts half-hidden in the undergrowth. Go past these along a narrow path between the stone wall and the backs of the gardens.

As you meet the road, go straight across down Myers Grove Lane, past the bottom of Ashurst Rd, onto a track. After 20 metres, turn left down the path to Little Matlock with views of Loxley valley in front.

As you pass the pleasing building that used to be the Robin Hood pub, turn left down the path immediately behind it.

Go straight down the path, which gets quite steep near the bottom, cross the footbridge turning right past the building, then right again at the lane. Carry on along this lovely little lane between the fields (having a chat with all the various animals if you wish) for about a kilometre until you reach some buildings with a high wall on your left.

As the lane bends up to the left, at the red brick, arch-windowed building on your left, take the path ahead down through the trees and then steps, to the right. As the path meanders on you will see still more industrial remains.

After about 400 metres you reach a fork in the path. Take the right path down the steps to a weir and Wisewood Forge Dam on the left. At the end of the dam follow the path to the right along the edge of the river with the new housing development behind the green fence on your left.

Eventually, you go through some girder barriers with an old industrial dam on the left. Go onward and back up to the road. Turn right, down the hill past the Yew Tree pub and straight ahead, leading back to Malin Bridge Tram terminus.

Further Information on this Walk

The Rivelin Valley:

http://www.rivelinvalley.org.uk/

WALK TWELVE

HERDINGS PARK
TO GRANVILLE ROAD

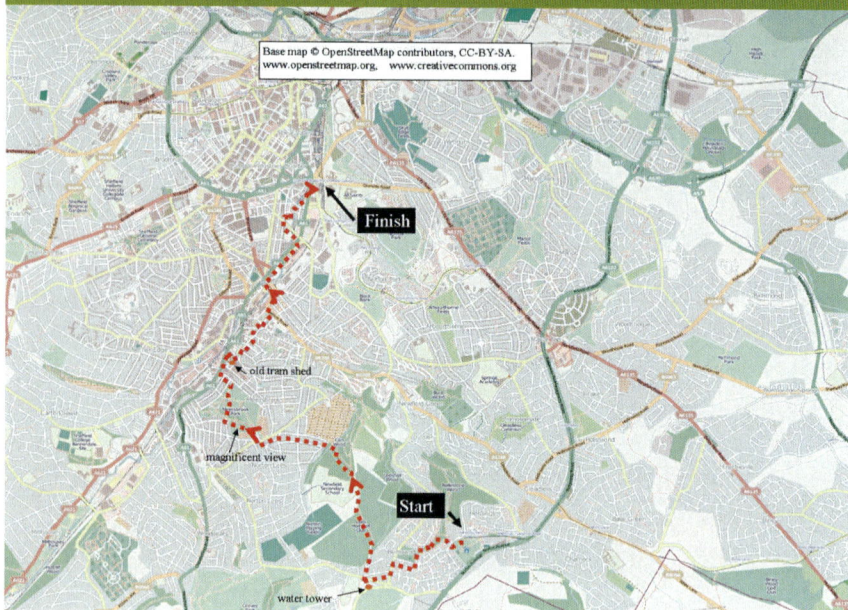

Base map © OpenStreetMap contributors, CC-BY-SA.
www.openstreetmap.org, www.creativecommons.org

Description

This is an urban walk through parks and golf courses and across ancient boundaries. You travel through transport history as well. There is the odd unsightly section but the really good news is that 95% of the walk is downhill and the view from Meersbrook Park is absolutely superb.

Start: Herdings Park Tram Terminus

Finish: Granville Road Tram Stop

Distance:
5 miles/
8 km

Time:
Allow 2½ hrs

Directions

Walk away from the terminus to the road and turn left. After about 80 metres, turn right down and past the end of Raeburn Close. At the rear of the houses there are three options, our route takes the path that leads diagonally left down into the woods (the Lumb) to the bottom, across what remains of a stream and up to the path at the rear of the houses ahead. Turn left along the path, behind the houses and along to the end, where the path turns right and up a few steps to the road.

Turn left here, up the hill for about 80 metres until the road starts to level out. Take the path to the left, past the end of Ironside Walk on your right and further along, with the playing fields on the same side. Carry on under the bridge and then immediately turn right, up the steps to the road, turning left along Constable Road to Blackstock Road.

Turn left up Blackstock Road and then second right into Backmoor Road, passing the picturesque and historic Nailmakers Arms on the right. Looming above the houses on your left you can see the Water Tower. As a child, I remember it being open to the public on Bank Holidays. My dad always claimed he could see Bombay on a clear day!

At the end of the road, turn right along Ashbury Lane. We are now following part of the extended Sheffield Round Walk. As the road ends, continue along the track, past the houses and down the side of Lees Hall Golf Course. After about 60 metres the main track bends away to the right. Don't follow it but take the smaller, left hand path through the green barrier along the edge of the course, where the views over the award-winning Gleadless Valley Housing estate come into view.

The grassy track now drops down along a hedged track between the golf course greens. Go straight down, ignoring several paths that join from both sides. The path veers to the right as it passes a school and its playing fields. At the bottom of the playing field, carry on straight through a metal

The lovely old Bishops' House

gate into the trees. At the bottom of the fence keep straight on and in 30 metres turn right up the track. Follow this for 50 metres then turn left at the cross-roads, as the path descends quickly into woods between two stone posts. Immediately past the posts, turn sharp left down the hill and left again as it meets a wider path.

Carry on down, over a footbridge and then up, with the allotments on the right. Turn right again shortly after these, up a short, steep section out onto Lees Hall Avenue. Go straight up here with the allotments still on your right, across the junction and down past some shops on the right to the main road.

Turn left up the main road to the brow of the hill with the lovely, old Bishop's House over the wall on your right. The Bishops' House is now used as a museum. Once past the House, turn right into Meersbrook Park, down past the trees to the open views – and you'll just have to stop.

The view is absolutely magnificent. There is no finer view over the city centre and its inner suburbs. There are plenty of benches to sit on, while you pick out the landmarks.

97

No finer view over the city

It's also worth remembering that the foot of the slope you are on used to be the boundary between Yorkshire and Derbyshire and perhaps, even in even more ancient times, between Mercia and Northumbria. Quite a significant spot.

Having enjoyed the rest, turn left along the path across the slope as it heads into the trees and, just as it reaches the backs of the houses, turn right and back out into the views again. Then take the right fork down, with the playground and then the dog-proof fenced area to the right. Turn left along Meersbrook Park Road past the Vestry Hall (now converted to student flats) to Chesterfield Road.

Turn right, and on the left as you cross the end of Valley Road, is the stone arch recess which used to contain a water trough. This was for the benefit of the hard-working horses as pulled the wagons, carts and later on, trams, up this section. Two roads further down, turn to the right up Albert Road. About 50 metres further, on the right, is the old tram shed entrance, now converted into apartments. You can just make out the engraving above the necessarily high doorway.

98

The old tram shed

Directly opposite this doorway, take the path up the slope and straight across the next road. The path then joins Goodwin Street. Carry on along the street and then the path across the next road, past a bouldering rock on your right. At the next road, turn up right for 30 metres then left, to pass a playground on your left. Across the next road go up towards and past Sheffield's own 'White Horse', cut out of the hillside, stopping for views across the valley to inner-city Abbeydale and beyond.

At the far end of the field you come out on Spencer Road. Go down this to Myrtle Road. Turn left over the railway and then right down Queens Road. Carry on down the road, over the meandering, urban River Sheaf to the next set of lights. On the right hand corner at this point there used to be one of the city's major depots for our previous tram system.

Turn left at the lights along Charlotte Road, past Priestley Road, over the river and then take the next right, down Edmund Road. As you reach the drill hall on the left, turn right down the short Rowsley Street to the bottom and then left along the side of the river behind the houses.

At the next road, cross over and continue along the riverside path until you come to Granville Square, just after

99

the anti-flooding sluice device where the river disappears under the roads. Cross Queens Road and walk up Granville Road to the tram stop.

Further Information on this Walk

Meersbrook Park:

https://www.sheffield.gov.uk/out--about/parks-woodlands--countryside/parks/a-z-city-district--local--parks/meersbrook-park.html

The Sheffield Tramway:

http://en.wikipedia.org/wiki/Sheffield_Tramway

WALK THIRTEEN
MEADOWHALL TO MEADOWHALL: THE CHALLENGE

Description

This is the ultimate test, based on a combination of:

Walk No. 7: Meadowhall to Middlewood

Walk No. 3: Middlewood to Halfway

Walk No. 5: Halfway to Meadowhall

The objective is to connect all three extremities of the tram network along one continuous path. It therefore means that you could start and finish at any of the three termini, but I have suggested Meadowhall as the base for a number of reasons:

First, since any start and finish would have to be at relatively unsociable hours, Meadowhall gives the best facilities for both access and refreshments.

Secondly, the initial section over to Middlewood is a relatively gentle breaking-in before the next gruelling section over the hills to Halfway. The final section will then seem like a piece of cake.

Third, the psychological boost of the prospect of somebody actually waiting for your return is more likely if they can pass the time lollopping around a shopping centre in relative comfort.

The time that I've suggested for the whole walk is more or less the sum of the times for the three separate sections with a little added on for the 'fatigue' factor. However, to make it more interesting, I suggest aiming to catch the first tram out and the last tram back which, as current timetables

**Distance:
41 miles/
65 km**

**Time:
Allow 18 hrs
(But see
Directions)**

go, would give you about 17 hours for the walk. Now there's a challenge!

One final comment on this walk: I have not done it myself! So, if anyone is sufficiently brave or foolhardy to have a go, I would be pleased to hear how they fared.

Start: At Meadowhall Interchange on Walk No. 7

Finish: At Meadowhall Interchange on Walk No. 5

Directions

Follow Walk No. 7 but, at the end, as you reach the road opposite Stockarth Lane don't carry on to the tram stop but cross directly over the road and up Stockarth Lane, carrying on Walk No. 3 from here, as shown in the map below:

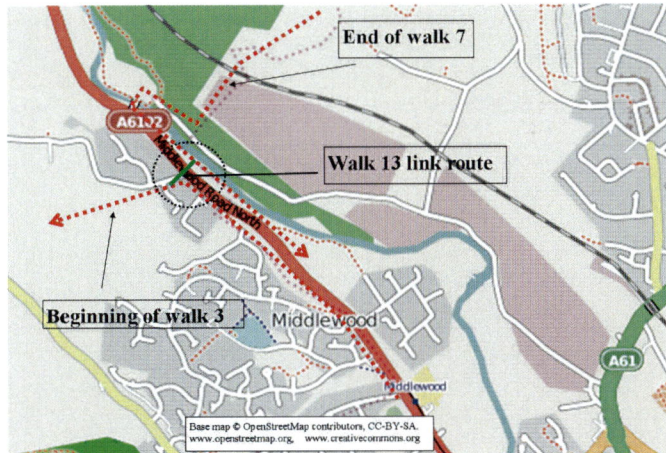

Near the end of Walk No. 3, you are walking down School Avenue. At the end, cross directly over the busy road and drop down to the left on the path behind the bus stop first to the left and then right down the side of the supermarket site, where you join the directions for Walk 5 as the path comes out at a road with factories on either side, as shown in the map below.

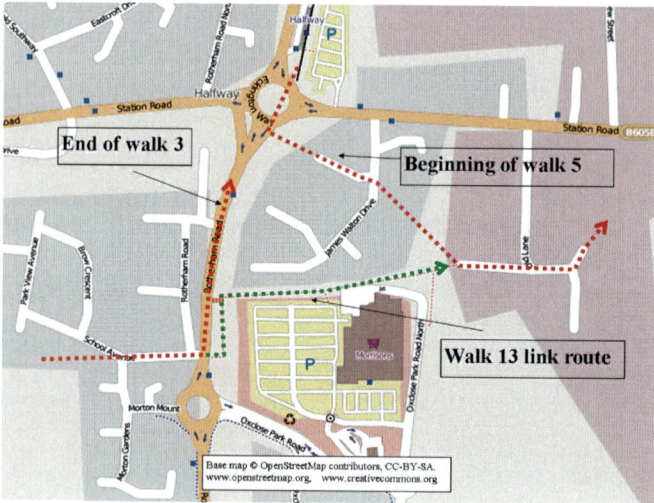